Mastering the MCAS in English Language Arts: Grade 10

STEVEN L. STERN

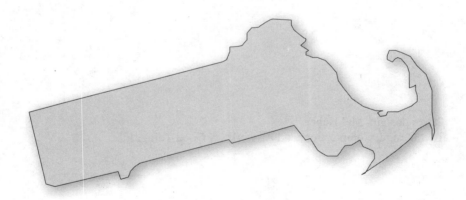

AMSCO

AMSCO SCHOOL PUBLICATIONS, INC.
315 HUDSON STREET, NEW YORK, NY 10013

About the Author

Steven L. Stern has 30 years of experience as a writer and textbook editor, developing a wide range of books, educational products, and informational materials for children and adults. He has written four other high school test-preparation books and is also the author of a novel as well as numerous articles and short stories. He has also worked as an English teacher, a lexicographer, and a writing consultant.

About the Reviewers

James E. McDermott, Ed.D. is the English/Language Arts Liaison in Worcester, MA where he continues to teach at least one English class at South High Community School. He began teaching in 1969 and has taught grades 7 through graduate school. He earned a BA in English Literature from the College of the Holy Cross, an MA in English Literature from Clark University, and an Ed. D. from Clark University. He is a former Massachusetts State Teacher of the Year.

George T. Viglirolo has been a Massachusetts public school teacher for nearly 30 years. He currently teaches at Brookline High School. In the past he has taught at City on a Hill Charter School in Boston, as well as at Saint Stephen's School in Rome, Italy. In addition, he is a member of the Massachusetts Assessment Development Committee.

This book is dedicated with love to my daughter Lisa and my son Michael.

Cover design: Mel Haber
Text Design, Composition, and Artwork: A Good Thing, Inc.

When ordering this book, please specify either **R710W** or Mastering the MCAS in English Language Arts: Grade 10

ISBN 1-56765-071-6

1 2 3 4 5 6 7 8 9 10   06 05 04 03 02 01 00

Contents

Introduction: The MCAS Test in English Language Arts

1-1	Overview of the test
1-2	Using This Book

"All words are pegs to hang ideas on."

Take a moment to consider the meaning of this statement, which was made by 19th century clergyman and writer Henry Ward Beecher. Beecher's observation applies to both reading and writing.

You have to think carefully about what you read in order to understand the author's ideas. As Beecher suggests, it's not the words, but the ideas behind them, that give writing its meaning. Similarly, when you write, you have to choose your words with care in order to get your point across.

The MCAS English Language Arts exam tests your ability to read with understanding and to express your ideas clearly through writing.

Part 1 presents a brief overview of the MCAS English Language Arts test. In this part, you'll also read a description of the organization and features of this book.

1-1 Overview of the Test

THE MCAS ENGLISH LANGUAGE ARTS EXAM

The MCAS exam has two parts: a Language and Literature portion and a Composition portion. Your score for the exam is based on your combined performance on both parts. *Preparing for the MCAS English Language Arts Exam* will help you get ready for the test by showing you what to expect, sharpening your reading, writing, and thinking skills, and giving you practice in applying these skills.

For the Language and Literature part of the exam, you will read a series of selections and answer multiple-choice questions about each selection. In addition, for most selections you will answer an open-response question. For a definition of two key terms, including *open-response question,* see the box on page 3.

MCAS Test in English Language Arts

Language and Literature portion
Read selections
Answer multiple-choice questions
Answer open-response questions

Composition portion
Write essay

The Composition part of the exam tests your writing skills. It also tests your ability to analyze literature. You'll be asked to write a clearly developed, well-organized essay that relates either to a work of literature that you've read or to a given reading passage.

Two Terms You Should Know

An **open-response question** asks you to reflect on a reading passage and then write a thoughtful response based on what you have read. Your response should be about one to two paragraphs long. It should include specific details or examples from the passage. Here's an example of an open-response question:

How does the author use imagery to create a mood? Support your answer with examples from the text.

A **prompt** consists of directions and information that explain specifically what you have to do for part of a test. In the Language and Literature part of the exam, each prompt identifies the source of a selection and usually includes information to help you understand the selection. In the Composition portion of the exam, the prompt defines the essay you have to write.

ACTIVITY: Reviewing Basics

Use your own words to answer the following questions. Write complete sentences.

1. What is an open-response question?

   _____

   _____

   _____

2. What is a prompt?

   _____

   _____

   _____

3. Explain how the Language and Literature portion of the exam and the Composition portion are different.

_____

_____

_____

1-2 Using This Book

CONTENT AND ORGANIZATION

This book is organized into five parts, and each part is divided into sections:

- Part 1, which you're reading now, is an introduction to the MCAS exam and to the content and features of this book.
- Part 2 provides test-taking strategies for the Language and Literature portion of the exam. This part includes three sections:

  Reading and Taking Notes
  Answering the Multiple-Choice Questions
  Answering the Open-Response Questions

- Part 3 focuses on reading and thinking skills you'll need to do well on the Language and Literature part of the exam. This part includes eight sections:

  Identifying Key Ideas and Information
  Making Inferences and Drawing Conclusions
  Understanding Cause and Effect
  Using Context Clues to Determine Meaning
  Understanding an Author's Purpose and Point of View
  Analyzing Elements of Fiction, Nonfiction, and Poetry
  Understanding Comparison and Contrast
  Answering Other Kinds of Questions

- Part 4 deals with the Composition portion of the exam. This part has two sections:

  Understanding the Writing Task
  Carrying Out the Writing Task

- Part 5 consists of a complete practice test.

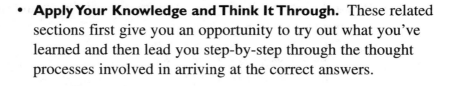

Overview of the Book

Part 1	Introduction
Part 2	Language and Literature portion of exam: test-taking strategies
Part 3	Language and Literature portion of exam: reading and thinking skills
Part 4	Composition portion of exam: essay writing
Part 5	Practice test

HELPFUL FEATURES

Parts 2-4 examine the prompts for each portion of the exam and the tasks associated with them. You'll learn key concepts and specific strategies and have many opportunities to apply and practice what you learn.

To cover a broad range of content in a way that is comprehensive yet easy to understand, this book contains a number of helpful features. For example, strategies are highlighted in dark type for quick reference and review. Various lists and diagrams clarify or emphasize important information. Other features include the following:

- **Activities.** Various activities throughout the book provide practice and reinforcement of what you learn. Most activities are intended for independent work. A few involve working with a partner or a small group of students.

- **Apply Your Knowledge and Think It Through.** These related sections first give you an opportunity to try out what you've learned and then lead you step-by-step through the thought processes involved in arriving at the correct answers.

- **Writing models.** Sample plans and responses based on the plans illustrate how to respond effectively to test prompts.

- **TIP boxes.** These appear throughout the book, providing useful tips for doing your best on the exam.
- **Boxed text.** Certain basic information is highlighted in separate boxes. For example, you'll see boxes about how to read poetry and how to tell fact from opinion.

- **Review summaries.** Brief summaries of key concepts and strategies appear at the end of Parts 2 and 4 and at the end of each section of Part 3.

- **Practice.** In addition to the complete test that appears in Part 5, practice test items appear at the end of Parts 2 and 4 and at the end of each section of Part 3.

PART TWO

MCAS Language and Literature: Test-Taking Strategies

> **2-1** Reading and Taking Notes
> **2-2** Answering the Multiple-Choice Questions
> **2-3** Answering the Open-Response Questions

"Knowledge is power."

Have you heard that saying? The English essayist and philosopher Francis Bacon wrote it in 1597. People continue to quote it today, because of its universal truth.

Your language arts knowledge and skills give you the power to do well on the MCAS English Language Arts exam. The test-taking strategies that you'll learn in this part of the book will help you use that power.

The Language and Literature portion of the MCAS English Language Arts exam consists of three related elements:

- reading passages
- multiple-choice questions
- open-response questions

The reading passages come from a variety of sources. Some passages are literary, while others are informational. Most of the reading selections are excerpts from longer works.

Where Do the Language and Literature Passages Come From?

Literary Works	Informational Works	
short stories	nonfiction books	speeches
novels	essays	editorials
poetry	letters	diary entries
plays	biographies	autobiographies
myths	interviews	newspaper
articles		
fables		

Reading selections often do not fit neatly into one category. A "literary" work may also convey information, while an "informational" work may tell an exciting story.

Both the multiple-choice questions and the open-response questions focus on important aspects of the reading passages. Some questions test your understanding of the text. Other questions test your knowledge of the techniques, structure, and elements of fiction and nonfiction.

In Part 2, you will learn basic strategies to help you read the Language and Literature passages and answer the questions. In Part 3, you will learn strategies to sharpen specific reading and thinking skills.

2-1 Reading and Taking Notes

LANGUAGE AND LITERATURE TEST ITEMS

The Language and Literature portion of the exam includes eight or nine reading passages. Each passage is introduced by a brief prompt. The prompt tells you the source of the selection and usually includes information to help you better understand what you read. Each reading passage is followed by four to eight multiple-choice questions. For most (but not all) passages, you also have to answer one open-response question.

Look at the typical test item that follows. For now, just look it over to get a feel for it. Do not read the selection yet. You will refer back to the prompt, the selection, and the questions later in this chapter.

In this excerpt from his book Gandhi: A Memoir, *William L. Shirer describes his first meeting, in 1931, with India's nationalist leader Mahatma Gandhi. Gandhi led the movement for Indian self-government, favoring nonviolence over violence to achieve independence from Great Britain. Read the excerpt carefully. When you have finished reading, answer the questions that follow.*

Gandhi: A Memoir
by William L. Shirer

A s our talk began I tried to take in not only what Gandhi was saying but how he looked. I had seen many photographs of him but I was nevertheless somewhat surprised at his actual appearance. His face at first glance did not convey at all the stature of the man, his obvious greatness. It was not one you would have especially noticed in a crowd. It struck me as not ugly, as some had said—indeed it radiated a certain beauty—but it was not uncommon either. Age—he was sixty-one—and fasting, an Indian

1   sun and the strain of years in prison, of long, hard nervous work, had obviously taken their toll, turned the nose down, widened it at the nostrils, sunk in his mouth just a little so that the lower lip protruded, and teeth were missing—I could see only two. His hair was closely cropped, giving

an effect of baldness. His large ears spread out, rabbitlike. His gray eyes lit up and sharpened when they peered at you through his steel-rimmed spectacles and then they softened when he lapsed, as he frequently did, into a mood of almost puckish humor. I was almost taken aback by the gaiety in them. This was a man inwardly secure, who, despite the burdens he carried, the hardships he had endured, could chuckle at man's foibles, including his own.

2   He seemed terribly frail, all skin and bones, though I knew that his appearance was deceptive, for he kept to a frugal but carefully planned diet that kept him fit, and for exercise he walked four or five miles each morning at a pace so brisk, as I would learn later when he invited me to accompany him, that I, at twenty-seven and in fair shape from skiing and hiking in the Alps below Vienna, could scarcely keep up. Over his skin and bones was a loosely wrapped *dhoti,* and in the chilliness of a north Indian winter he draped a coarsely spun white shawl over his bony shoulders. His skinny legs were bare, his feet in wooden sandals.

3   As he began to talk, his voice seemed high-pitched, but his words were spoken slowly and deliberately and with emphasis when he seemed intent on stressing a point, and gradually, as he warmed up, the tone lowered. His slightly accented English flowed rhythmically, like a poet's at times, and always, except for an occasional homespun cliché, it was concise, homely, forceful.

4   For so towering a figure, his humble manner at first almost disconcerted me. Most of the political greats I had brushed up against in Europe and at home had seemed intent on impressing you with the forcefulness of their personalities and the boldness of their minds, not being bashful at all in hiding their immense egos. But here was the most gentle and unassuming of men, speaking softly and kindly, without egotism, without the slightest pretense of trying to impress his rather awed listener.

5   How could so humble a man, I wondered, spinning away with his nimble fingers on a crude wheel as he talked, have begun almost single-handedly to rock the foundations of the British Empire, aroused a third of a billion people to rebellion against foreign rule, and taught them the technique of a new revolutionary method—non-violent civil disobedience—against which Western guns and Eastern lathis were proving of not much worth? That was what I had come to India to find out. So I simply said:

6   "How have you done it?"

7   "By love and truth," he smiled. "In the long run no force can prevail against them."

Multiple-Choice Questions

1. This excerpt is written in which person?

   A. first

   B. second

   C. third

   D. fourth

2. What does the author mean in paragraph 2 when he writes: "He seemed terribly frail, all skin and bones, though I knew that this appearance was deceptive"?

   A. Gandhi pretended to be in better physical condition than he was.

   B. Gandhi was stronger than he appeared.

   C. Gandhi's diet had caused his health to suffer.

   D. Gandhi used his appearance to gain people's sympathy.

3. This excerpt is an example of

   A. autobiography.

   B. persuasive writing.

   C. satire.

   D. biography.

4. Which word is closest to the meaning of *disconcerted* in paragraph 4?

   A. amused

   B. enraged

   C. confused

   D. saddened

5. Unlike most other political leaders the author had met, Gandhi

    A. was an insecure person.

    B. did not try to impress him.

    C. was very young.

    D. could not speak English.

6. Why did the author come to India?

    A. to join the movement for Indian independence

    B. to learn how Gandhi had so greatly affected India's people

    C. to gather information about Gandhi's diet and exercise program

    D. to photograph Gandhi

7. The phrase "rock the foundations of the British Empire" in paragraph 5 is an example of

    A. a simile.

    B. a metaphor.

    C. onomatopoeia.

    D. personification.

8. The tone of this excerpt suggests that the author views Gandhi with

    A. admiration.

    B. distrust.

    C. contempt.

    D. pity.

Open-Response Questions

9. Describe two ways that Gandhi turned out to be different from what William Shirer had expected. Support your answer with specific information from the excerpt.

_____

_____

_____

_____

_____

_____

_____

_____

As you look over the introductory prompt, notice how it prepares you to read the passage. In this case, the prompt gives you several helpful pieces of information:

- The passage is an excerpt from the book *Gandhi: A Memoir* by William L. Shirer.
- The passage describes the author's first meeting with Mahatma Gandhi.
- "Gandhi led the movement for Indian self-government, favoring nonviolence over violence to achieve independence from Great Britain."

ACTIVITY A: Examining Prompts

Two Language and Literature prompts appear below. Read each prompt and answer the questions.

Prompt 1: *The following selection is an excerpt from the novel* Of Mice and Men *by American novelist John Steinbeck. This scene occurs as the two main characters, George and Lennie, first meet Curley, the son of the boss. Read the excerpt and then answer the questions that follow.*

1. What information does the prompt give you? Be specific.

   _____

   _____

   _____

2. How will this information help you when you read
   the passage?

   _____

   _____

   _____

Prompt 2: *The following selection contains instructions for
following a biking route through central Massachusetts.
Read the instructions carefully. Then answer the
questions that follow.*

3. Do you think the selection that follows this prompt will be
   fiction or nonfiction? What makes you think so?

   _____

   _____

   _____

STRATEGIES FOR ACTIVE READING

Reading is an *active* process—a process that requires thought and
concentration. Here are some strategies to help you read the
Language and Literature passages actively.

- **Get information from the prompt.** Read the introduction
  carefully. What information does it give you? For example, is
  the reading passage an excerpt or a complete work? Is it
  fiction or nonfiction? What does the prompt tell you about
  the author?
- **Read the passage more than once.** In general, read each
  passage at least twice before answering the questions. Reading
  a passage more than once will increase your comprehension.
  For specific tips on reading poetry, study the box on page 17.
- **Skim the questions in advance.** The reason you're reading
  the passage is to be able to answer the multiple-choice and
  open-response questions that follow. So, *before* reading the
  passage, or between your first and second readings, take time

to look over the questions. Skimming them in advance will alert you to important ideas and information to watch for as you read.

- **Be a careful, thoughtful reader.** Consider why the author is writing—what is his or her purpose? Try to identify the main ideas that the author wants to communicate. Keep in mind that some ideas may be stated, while others may only be implied. Watch for key facts and details. Also think about the title of the passage, which may offer clues to the meaning of the passage.

- **Think about difficult sections.** Don't be tempted to skip over parts of a passage that you don't immediately understand. Instead, reread the text—several times, if necessary—and try to grasp its meaning. Use the *context* (the words that come before and after) to help you figure out the meaning of a particular word, phrase, or sentence.

- **Consider the elements of fiction and nonfiction.** Be aware of how an author is using the elements of fiction and nonfiction to get his or her ideas across. You'll learn more about the elements of fiction and nonfiction in Part 3, pages 53-208.

- **Take notes.** Jotting down important points can help you understand the reading passages. The next section of this chapter contains suggestions for taking notes.

BE AN	→	*Concentrate* on what you're reading.
ACTIVE	→	*Think about* ideas and information.
READER	→	*Jot down* key points.

Reading Poetry

- Always read a poem several times. Read slowly. Think about the words and images.
- Consider the kind of poem you're reading. Does it tell a story? Express an emotion? Describe a scene?
- Identify important ideas, stated *and* implied.
- Look for multiple levels of meaning, often conveyed through the poet's figurative or symbolic use of words.
- Reread difficult lines and try to figure out their meaning. Use context clues to help you determine the meaning of unfamiliar words or phrases.
- Restate or summarize the poet's ideas in your own words.

TIP: Build Your Vocabulary

The bigger your vocabulary, the more words you have at your command when you read, write, or speak. Here are a few suggestions to help you build your vocabulary:

- Read! Spend time every day reading newspapers, magazines, and/or books.
- When you read or hear a word you don't know, look it up in a dictionary. Don't just skip it.
- Keep a list of new words that you learn. Try to use them in written and oral communication.
- Look for other ways to expand your vocabulary. For example, use a word-a-day desk calendar or a vocabulary-builder study book.

NOTE-TAKING TIPS

Although you don't have to take notes for the Language and Literature reading passages, doing so works to your benefit. Besides helping you understand what you read, notes can help you find the information you'll need to answer the questions—especially the open-response questions.

The notes that you take can be much, much simpler than notes you take for school. In fact, your goal is to write as little as possible but enough to make your notes useful. Because the reading selections are generally short and you can refer back to them, *your notes need serve only as a kind of road map to important ideas and information.* For some passages, you may want to take many notes. For others, such as those not followed by an open-response question, you may decide not to take any notes at all. Use your judgment.

For poetry and very short selections, you're usually best off reading the whole passage once or twice before taking notes. For other passages, you may want to jot down some notes even during your first reading. Use whatever note-taking approach you feel comfortable with and works well for you. Here are some other suggestions.

- **Be brief and clear.** Zero in on *the most important* ideas and information. Write words and phrases, not whole sentences. Make your notes as short and simple as you can without losing meaning.

- **Include paragraph numbers in your notes.** You'll need to refer back to the passage as you answer the questions. Noting which paragraph in a reading passage contains a particular item will help you locate that item quickly, especially if the selection is more than a few paragraphs long.

- **Use a loose outline form.** For some passages, you may want to organize your notes paragraph by paragraph. For others, you may prefer to organize your notes around important ideas. Often, you may choose to combine both approaches. Do whatever works best—there's no rule. Compare the examples below.

Loose outline: paragraph by paragraph	**Loose outline: important ideas**

Paragraph 1
   Main idea
     —supporting detail
     —supporting detail
	First important idea
	     —supporting detail
	     —supporting detail

Paragraph 2
   Main idea
     —supporting detail
     —supporting detail
	Second important idea
	     —supporting detail
	     —supporting detail

Make your notes easy to follow by writing ideas at the left margin and indenting supporting information beneath them. Precede each supporting detail with a dash or, when appropriate, a number.

Leave space before starting a new idea, in case you want to add information. Also leave wide margins on both sides of your notes.

- **Make note of ideas and details that relate to questions you're going to have to answer.** Jot down relevant information, even when it doesn't fit in neatly with your outline. For example, suppose that an open-response question asks you to discuss an author's use of imagery. As you read the passage, make note of any striking images and where they appear.

- **Use shortcuts.** Shorten words and use abbreviations and symbols such as these:

+	and	e.g.	for example
B4	before	$	money
Info	information	%	percent
w/	with	w/o	without

Also, write numerals rather than spell out numbers.

- **Highlight notes of special importance.** Underline or circle key words, or print them in capital letters. You may also find it helpful to underline important points in the reading selection itself. Just don't get carried away and underline *too* many lines.

APPLY YOUR KNOWLEDGE

Let's see how the suggestions you've read can be put into practice.

- Read the prompt, the selection, and questions 1-9 on pages 11-15. Use the reading strategies on pages 16-18.
- When you've finished reading, look again at the first two paragraphs of the selection, shown below. Re-read the paragraphs and compare them with the sample student notes.

Keep in mind that these notes are only an example. Your own notes for these paragraphs might be somewhat different.

- Think about these questions:
  - How are the notes organized?
  - What information does the student include? Why?
  - What shortcuts does the student use?
- Read *Think It Through,* on the next page.

Gandhi: A Memoir
by William L. Shirer

As our talk began I tried to take in not only what Gandhi was saying but how he looked. I had seen many photographs of him but I was nevertheless somewhat surprised at his actual appearance. His face at first glance did not convey at all the stature of the man, his obvious greatness. It was not one you would have especially noticed in a crowd. It struck me as not ugly, as some had said—indeed it radiated a certain beauty—but it was not uncommon either. Age—he was sixty-one—and fasting, an Indian

Author surprised by G's looks (P1)
—face doesn't convey "greatness"
—"gaiety" in his eyes
G = 61 years old
G "inwardly secure" (P1)

1   sun and the strain of years in prison, of long, hard nervous work, had obviously taken their toll, turned the nose down, widened it at the nostrils, sunk in his mouth just a little so that the lower lip protruded, and teeth were missing—I could see only two. His hair was closely cropped, giving an effect of baldness. His large ears spread out, rabbitlike. His gray eyes lit up and sharpened when they peered at you through his steel-rimmed spectacles and then they softened when he lapsed, as he frequently did, into a mood of almost puckish humor. I was almost taken aback by the gaiety in them. This was a man inwardly secure, who, despite the burdens he carried, the hardships he had endured, could chuckle at man's foibles, including his own.

He seemed terribly frail, all skin and bones, though I knew that his appearance was deceptive, for he kept to a frugal but carefully planned diet that kept him fit, and for exercise he walked four or five miles each morning at a pace so brisk, as I would learn later when he invited me to

2   accompany him, that I, at twenty-seven and in fair shape from skiing and hiking in the Alps below Vienna, could scarcely keep up. Over his skin and bones was a loosely wrapped *dhoti,* and in the chilliness of a north Indian winter he draped a coarsely spun white shawl over his bony shoulders. His skinny legs were bare, his feet in wooden sandals.

G keeps fit (P2)
—diet
—exercise
—author "could scarcely keep up" on walks

Think It Through

As you compare the notes with the actual text, you'll note several important points:

- The notes are very brief. The student included only ideas and details that seemed most important and relevant.
- The notes are concise. The student wrote in phrases, not whole sentences. The student also shortened or abbreviated words—for example, *G* for "Gandhi," *looks* for "appearance."
- The student used quotation marks to identify certain key words and phrases from the passage.
- The student used a loose outline form. Paragraph numbers *(P1, P2)* will make it easy to find important information in the passage.
- Skimming the questions in advance helped guide the student's notes. For example, having read question 9, the open-response question, the student was on the lookout for "ways that Gandhi turned out to be different from what William Shirer had expected." Therefore, the student noted this idea: "Author surprised by G's looks (P1)."

- The student jotted down details relating directly to questions, even when these details did not fit in neatly with the outline. For example:

  G = 61 years old

  G "inwardly secure" (P1)

Be specific in your answer: How would the two lines of notes above help you answer question 5?

_____

_____

_____

_____

Activity B: Reading and Taking Notes

Read and take notes for the selection on pages 11-12. (For paragraphs 1 and 2, you can take your own notes or adapt the sample student notes that appear above.) Use the strategies you've learned for reading and taking notes.

    Save your notes. You will refer back to them later in this chapter.

Activity C: Improving Note-Taking Skills

Pair up with another student. Exchange the notes you took for *Activity B* and evaluate each other's work. Be constructive and specific in your comments and suggestions. Try to help your partner improve his or her skills. Here are some guidelines.

- Do the notes focus on the selection's *most important* and *relevant* ideas and information? What ideas and information should be included but are not?
- Are the notes brief and clear? How could they be improved?
- Are the notes useful? In particular, will the notes be helpful in answering the open-response question? How could the notes be made more useful?

2-2 Answering the Multiple-Choice Questions

STRATEGIES FOR ANSWERING THE QUESTIONS

The multiple-choice questions that follow the reading passages cover a wide range of content. These questions test your knowledge of language and literature as well as your reading and thinking skills. To answer the questions, you'll use the strategies you've learned for reading and taking notes. In Part 3 of this book, you'll learn additional skills that will help you answer the questions.

There are two types of multiple-choice questions on the exam: question and answer and sentence completion. Both types offer four answer choices. Here's an example of each type:

Question and answer:

Which is the most likely reason that Michael returned home?

   A. He ran out of money.

   B. The weather became stormy.

   C. He missed his family.

   D. The people he met frightened him.

Sentence completion:

According to the author, the primary purpose of literature is to

   A. entertain readers.

   B. educate the public.

   C. inspire people.

   D. persuade readers.

Use the following strategies to help you answer the multiple-choice questions.

- **Read each question carefully.** Be sure you understand the *question* before you consider the answers.

To answer question-and-answer-type questions, think about what the answer *should* be before you look at the choices. To answer sentence-completion-type questions, try rereading the question with each possible answer.

- **Identify key words in the question that point you toward the correct answer.** For example, in the following question, the word *primary* is a key word. It tells you to look not for just any reason, but for the primary, or main, reason:

  What was the primary reason that the candidate lost the election?

Pay special attention to words that are in **bold** type. These words directly affect your answer choice. For example, in the following questions, how would the boldfaced word help you choose the correct answer?

> What does the author miss **most** about city life?
> What is the **main** purpose of this article?
> The road leads past all of the following **except.**
> Which is **not** a reason why cats are popular pets?

- **Refer back to the reading passage as often as necessary and use your notes to help you.** For poetry and plays, in particular, you may need to reread certain lines several times in order to answer a question.
- **Use the context.** If a question refers to a specific paragraph, review that paragraph before trying to answer. You may also need to look at the preceding or following paragraph.

For literary selections, be ready to use context clues to help you find an author's *implied* meaning. For example, context clues can help you analyze poetic images. And don't rush to answer: re-read the relevant text and think about it before making an answer choice. You'll learn more about using context clues in Part 3 (pages 53-208).

- **Read, compare, and consider *all* the choices. Then pick the best and most complete answer.** This advice is especially important for literary passages, because questions may deal with multiple levels of meaning, and the differences between answer choices may be subtle. Also, for questions about elements of fiction and nonfiction, choose your answer carefully. Don't, for example, confuse similes with metaphors or autobiography with biography.
- **Narrow your search.** If you're not sure which answer is correct, cross out choices you know are *incorrect.* Then concentrate on just the remaining choices.

- **Don't get stuck on a difficult question.** Make your best choice and move on. If you have time left over, you can go back to the troublesome question. Also, you'll sometimes find that answering one question helps you answer another.
- **Answer every question.**

APPLY YOUR KNOWLEDGE

- Review the prompt and the selection on pages 11-12. Also review the notes you took for *Activity B,* on page 22.
- Next, answer multiple-choice questions 1–8 on pages 13-14.
- After you've answered the questions, read *Think It Through* below to see how one student determined the correct answers.

Think It Through

1. This excerpt is written in which person?

    A. first

    B. second

    C. third

    D. fourth

    The narrator himself is telling the story in this excerpt. I know that this is called *first-person* point of view. Works written in the first person use pronouns like *I, me,* and *my.* Choice A is the correct answer.

2. What does the author mean in paragraph 2 when he writes: "He seemed terribly frail, all skin and bones, though I knew that this appearance was deceptive."?

    A. Gandhi pretended to be in better physical condition than he was.

    B. Gandhi was stronger than he appeared.

    C. Gandhi's diet had caused his health to suffer.

    D. Gandhi used his appearance to gain people's sympathy.

First, I review paragraph 2, so I can see the whole context. The paragraph tells me that Gandhi was in good physical condition, even though he didn't look it. Therefore, choice B is correct. However, I consider all the other choices, to be safe. Based on the passage, none is true, so choice B must be right.

3. This excerpt is an example of

   A. autobiography.
   B. persuasive writing.
   C. satire.
   D. biography.

I can eliminate choices B and C, because neither one applies to the passage. I know that autobiographies and biographies both tell the story of a person's life. However, an autobiography is written by the person himself or herself. Since this excerpt is about Gandhi but is written by someone else, I know that it's a biography, choice D.

4. Which word is closest to the meaning of *disconcerted* in paragraph 4?

   A. amused
   B. enraged
   C. confused
   D. saddened

First, I review paragraph 4. The main idea is that Gandhi's "humble manner" makes him surprisingly different from other "political greats" the author has met. I also look at paragraph 5. I see that the author is trying to understand how "so humble a man" could be so powerful. With this context, I can conclude that the word closest in meaning to disconcerted is "confused," choice C.

5. Unlike most other political leaders the author had met, Gandhi

A. was an insecure person.

B. did not try to impress him.

C. was very young.

D. could not speak English.

Paragraph 5 (especially the last sentence) tells me that the

correct answer is choice B. Also, the notes I took while reading

help me eliminate two choices:

G = 61 years old ⟵ *61 is not "very young"—this eliminates choice C*

G "inwardly secure" (P1) ⟵ *not "insecure"—this eliminates choice A*

I know that choice D is wrong, too, because paragraph 3

mentions Gandhi's "slightly accented English."

6. Why did the author come to India?

A. to join the movement for Indian independence

B. to learn how Gandhi had so greatly affected India's people

C. to gather information about Gandhi's diet and exercise program

D. to photograph Gandhi

The next-to-last sentence of paragraph 5—That was what I had

come to India to find out—suggests that the answer to the

question must be in this paragraph. After carefully rereading the

paragraph, I conclude that choice B is correct. Besides, I can

also see that none of the other choices is supported by

the text.

7. The phrase "rock the foundations of the British Empire" in paragraph 5 is an example of

A. a simile.

B. a metaphor.

C. onomatopoeia.

D. personification.

The author is comparing Gandhi's effect on the British Empire with physical force. I know that both similes and metaphors are methods of comparison. However, a simile uses like or as, while a metaphor does not. Therefore, choice B is correct.

8. The tone of this excerpt suggests that the author views Gandhi with

A. admiration

B. distrust

C. contempt

D. pity

I know that tone is the attitude an author shows toward his or her subject. The author's attitude toward Gandhi is positive and admiring throughout this excerpt. (In fact, at the end of paragraph 4, the author even says he's "awed.") Therefore, I'm sure that choice A is correct.

Activity D: Building Your Skills

Review the notes you took and the multiple-choice questions you answered. Then answer the following questions. Be as specific as you can.

1. How useful were your notes? How could you have made them more useful?

_____

_____

_____

2. Which multiple-choice questions did you find most challenging to answer? Why? What could you do to make answering such questions easier?

_____

_____

_____

3. Did you read the selection carefully enough? What could you have done to improve your understanding of the text?

_____

_____

_____

4. Share and compare your answers to the preceding questions with the answers of other students. What suggestions from other students did you find helpful?

_____

_____

_____

2-3 Answering the Open-Response Questions

THOUGHTFUL WRITTEN RESPONSES

In some ways the multiple-choice questions and the open-response questions are alike. Both cover a wide range of content, and both require you to apply the strategies discussed in Parts 2 and 3 of this book.

However, a multiple-choice question asks you to *choose* an answer, whereas an open-response question asks you to *create* one. Specifically, for each open-response question, you will have to write a response that is about one to two paragraphs long.

The open-response questions take various forms. Compare the five sample questions below. How are they alike? How do they differ?

How does the author use imagery to create a mood? Support your answer with examples from the text.

Based on this scene, describe how the characters feel about the king. Use examples from the play to support your answers.

Why is the study of history important? Use information from the speech to explain the reasons.

How has the narrator's attitude toward people changed over the years? Why? Use specific evidence from the excerpt to support your answer.

What does the author say about each person's responsibilities in a free society? Give examples of how a citizen can live up to these responsibilities.

As you can see, open-response questions do not fit any one pattern. What they have in common is that they all require you to reflect on the reading passage and then write a thoughtful response based on what you've read.

Fill in the blanks: Your response to an open-response question should be about _____ to _____ paragraphs in length.

Scoring Guidelines

Overall, your written responses will be evaluated on the basis of two criteria:

- your understanding of the reading selection
- your understanding of the techniques, structure, and elements of different types of literature

Furthermore, the readers who score your responses will be guided by criteria specific for each *individual* open-response question. For example, for one question, readers may evaluate how well you understand the theme of a passage. For another question, readers may focus on your interpretation of the symbolism used in a passage.

However, one scoring guideline will apply to each and every open-response question: Readers will always look at how well you support your answer with specific information, details, or examples from the passage.

In fact, if you look again at the five sample questions on page 30, you'll see that every one makes reference to the use of supporting information or examples. As a rule of thumb, the more detail—specific and relevant detail—that you include from the passage to support your answer, the higher your score will be.

TIP: Use the Number of Paragraphs You Need

To answer an open-response question, write as many paragraphs as you need to present your ideas clearly. For some questions, you'll find that a single paragraph does the job. For other questions, you may need to write two or even three paragraphs.

Keep in mind, too, that no one approach works for every question. Sometimes you'll want to answer a question in one long paragraph. Other times, two short paragraphs will be more effective. Choose the approach that you think works best.

STRATEGIES FOR ANSWERING THE QUESTIONS

The first three strategies that you learned for answering multiple-choice questions will also work for answering open-response questions:

- **Read each question carefully.** Be sure you understand exactly what the question is asking.
- **Identify key words in the question.** For open-response questions, the key words are often verbs, such as *describe* or *explain.* These words are important because they help to define your specific writing task.

Also watch for numbers. For instance, some questions ask you to include "two examples." Most questions, however, don't specify. They simply tell you to support your answer with "examples," "information," or "detailed evidence." As a general rule, it's always wise to develop a main idea with *at least two* supporting details or examples.

- **Refer back to the reading passage as often as necessary and use your notes to help you.** In addition, you can refer back to the multiple-choice questions. They often focus on important ideas or information that you may want to include when you answer the open-response question.

Complete the sentence: For every open-response question, readers will look to see how well you support your answer with

_____

_____

How to Plan and Write a Response

Answering an open-response question is like writing a short essay. First, you have to plan what points you want to communicate. Then you have to express those points clearly in writing.

To answer an open-response question, follow these five steps:

1. Make a plan.
2. State your main idea(s).
3. Support your idea(s).
4. Reread what you've written.
5. Proofread your work.

Let's take a closer look at each step.

Step 1: Make a plan. After reading and thinking about the question, don't just start writing. Take time to plan before you write.

First, decide what your main idea is—that is, the main point that you're going to make in response to the question.

Second, jot down specific and relevant details from the reading passage to support your main idea. Supporting information may include facts, examples, reasons, or words quoted directly from the passage. For tips on using quotation marks, study the box on page 43.

Third, number the supporting details in the order you plan to write about them. You can change your mind later, but numbering the details at the start will help you organize your thoughts.

> Main idea (your answer to the question)
>
> 1 -supporting detail
>
> 2 -supporting detail
>
> 3 -supporting detail

If you want to present more than one main idea in your response, jot down and number supporting details for *each* of your ideas.

Step 2: State your main idea(s). Clearly express your main idea in a topic sentence. For tips on writing topic sentences for open-response questions, study the box on page 35.

Often you can reshape the question itself to create your topic sentence. Here are two examples based on questions you saw earlier. Notice how each topic sentence repeats many of the same words that appear in the question.

Question:	Based on this scene, describe how the characters feel about the king. Use examples from the play to support your answers.
Topic sentence:	Based on the scene, the characters feel both love and respect for the king.
Question:	Why is the study of history important? Use information from the speech to explain the reasons.
Topic sentence:	The study of history is important because people can learn from mistakes that were made in the past.

Reshape this question to create a topic sentence:

How does a student's attitude toward school change once the student enters high school? Support your answer with specific examples.

_____

_____

_____

_____

If you want to organize your response around more than one main idea, express each one in a topic sentence. For example, you could write a one-paragraph response around this topic sentence:

Based on the scene, the characters feel great admiration for the king.

Or you could organize the same response into two paragraphs around these two topic sentences:

(1) Based on the scene, the characters feel great love for the king.

(2) In addition to love, the characters feel respect for the king.

Step 3: Support your idea(s). After stating your main idea in a topic sentence, develop the idea with your supporting details. *Write as many sentences as you need to explain your point clearly and completely.*

Be sure that every main idea you present is adequately supported with specific and relative details.

Step 4: Reread what you've written. Check that you have answered the question clearly, specifically, and completely. Adjust or expand your response as needed.

Step 5: Proofread your work. Correct any mistakes in grammar, punctuation, capitalization, and spelling.

Writing Topic Sentences For Open-Response Questions

Do:

write a topic sentence that answers the question and clearly
    states your main idea

write a topic sentence that serves as an introductory statement
    for your supporting information

Don't:

make your topic sentence too broad, general, or vague.

make your topic sentence so narrow that you can't develop it
    with supporting information.

Compare these examples:

Open-response question:

> What does the unicorn in the story symbolize? Use specific
> evidence from the excerpt to support your answer.

Effective topic sentence:

> The unicorn in this story symbolizes both independence and
> freedom.

Too general and vague:

> The unicorn in this story stands for other things.

Too narrow to be a topic sentence:

> The unicorn in the story escapes into the forest.

Activity E: Making a Plan

Review the prompt, the selection, and questions 1–9 on pages 11-15.
Also review the notes you took for *Activity B,* on page 22. Then
make a plan for answering question 9, the open-response question:

9. Describe two ways that Gandhi turned out to be different from what William Shirer had expected. Support your answer with specific information from the excerpt.

Follow the guidelines above for *Step 1: Make a Plan.*

_____

_____

_____

_____

_____

_____

_____

_____

_____

_____

_____

Activity F: Comparing Plans

Pair up with another student. Compare the plans you made for *Activity E.* Discuss the following questions. Be constructive and specific in your comments.

1. What are the main differences between your two plans?

_____

_____

_____

2. What are the strengths of each plan?

_____

_____

_____

_____

3. How could each plan be improved?

_____

_____

_____

Looking at a Sample Plan

Let's see how one student made a plan to answer the open-response question about the Gandhi excerpt. Look at the sample plan below. You'll probably find that it's similar to the plan you made for *Activity E.*

Later in this chapter, you'll see how the student used this plan to answer the open-response question.

Student's Plan for Open-Response Question

<u>Note:</u> For illustration purposes, this plan may be more detailed than yours would need to be. Your plan needs to have only enough detail for <u>you</u> to understand what you intend to write!

Gandhi <u>different in appearance and physical condition</u> from what Shirer expected

1 —G's looks not special—"did not convey . . . greatness"

2 —"gaiety" in eyes despite responsibilities and hardships

3 —G "seemed terribly frail"—but turned out to be in such good shape, Shirer "could scarcely keep up" on walks

Gandhi also <u>different in his manner</u> from expected

1 —humble, didn't try to impress others-"gentle and unassuming"

2 —spoke "softly and kindly, without egotism"

Activity G: Evaluating a Plan

Answer the following questions about the student's plan. Before writing your answers, discuss your thoughts with a partner or a small group of students.

1. Overall, what are the strengths of the plan?

_____

_____

_____

2. What are the two main ideas around which the student plans to organize the response?

_____

_____

_____

3. Explain how the details that the student has included will support the main ideas.

_____

_____

_____

4. How did answering the multiple-choice questions help the student make the plan?

_____

_____

_____

Activity H: Comparing Plans

Carefully compare the sample plan above with the plan you made for *Activity E* (page 35). Then answer the following questions.

1. How are the two plans different?

_____

_____

_____

2. In what ways do you think your plan may be better than the sample plan? Be specific.

_____

_____

_____

3. In what ways might the sample plan be stronger than yours? Again, be specific.

_____

_____

_____

Translating a Plan Into a Response

If you carefully plan your answer to an open-response question, you'll find that writing goes smoothly. Keep in mind that your plan is *flexible.* You can make changes and adjustments as you write.

Let's see how the student translated the plan on page 37 into a response. First, review the plan. Then read the student's answer that appears on the next page.

9. Describe two ways that Gandhi turned out to be different from what William Shirer had expected. Support your answer with specific information from the excerpt.

> Gandhi's appearance and physical condition turned out to be different from what William Shirer had expected. First, as great a man as Gandhi was, there was nothing special about his looks. Shirer says that Gandhi's face was "not uncommon" and would not stand out in a crowd. Second, Shirer thought that Gandhi looked very frail, but he later found out that he "could scarcely keep up" with Gandhi on walks.
>
> Gandhi also turned out to be different than expected in his manner. Shirer had not expected someone so humble. He had thought that Gandhi might try to impress him, like other "political greats" Shirer had known. However, Gandhi was "gentle and unassuming" and did not seem to have a big ego.

Notice how the student's plan guided the structure and content of the response. Each paragraph is based on a main idea, stated in a topic sentence. The student supported each main idea with specific, relevant details.

The response has a clear and logical flow. The student used the transitional words *first, second,* and *however* to connect ideas. You'll learn more about transitional words and phrases in Part 4 of this book.

Note that sometimes the student did *not* exactly follow the original plan.

- The student included most, but not all, of the information in the plan. For example, the student decided that the "gaiety" detail wasn't really necessary and omitted it. The student also omitted the detail about speaking "softly and kindly."
- The student adjusted and expanded the plan wording as needed. Compare, for example, the following detail with the corresponding sentence in the response:

Plan detail:

G's looks not special—"did not convey . . . greatness"

Response:

. . . as great a man as Gandhi was, there was nothing

special about his looks.

- The student did not limit the response to only what was in the plan. For example, the response includes four direct quotations from the excerpt to support the main ideas. Two of these quotations appeared in the plan, but the other two did not.

  <u>Note:</u> When you write an answer to an open-response question, you'll often want to go back to the selection for additional information.

Activity 1: Examining a Response

Answer the following questions about the student's response.

1. In what ways do you think planning before writing helped the student write the response?

   _____

   _____

   _____

2. Do you agree with the student's decision not to include in the response all the details that were in the plan? Give reasons for your answer and refer to at least two specific examples.

   _____

   _____

   _____

3. You read on page 40 how "the student adjusted and expanded the plan wording as needed." Give one example of this (not the same one as on page 40), and explain why you think the student made the change.

_____

_____

_____

_____

4. Review the box on page 35, *Writing Topic Sentences for Open-Response Questions*. How well do the student's two topic sentences follow the guidelines? Be specific.

_____

_____

_____

Activity J: Learning From Experience

Review the notes that you took for *Activity B* on page 21. Then work with a partner or a small group of students to answer the following question.

Based on what you've learned about planning and writing a response, list two specific suggestions for making the notes you take as useful as possible for answering open-response questions.

1. _____

_____

_____

2. _____

_____

_____

Using Quotation Marks

- Use quotation marks to set off a direct quotation—the exact words of a writer or speaker. Do *not* use quotation marks with an indirect quotation—a restatement, or *paraphrase,* of a writer's or speaker's words.

Direct quotation:	"People must take responsibility for their actions," the governor said.
Indirect quotation:	The governor said that people should accept responsibility for what they do.
Direct quotation:	The author describes Lisa as "a woman who prizes honesty above all else."
Indirect quotation:	The author says that Lisa highly values honesty.

- Always place commas and periods at the end of a quotation *inside* the quotation marks.

  "Learn from the past," the author writes.
  The author urges readers to "learn from the past."

- When you want to leave out words from a quotation, use an ellipsis (...) to show that words are omitted.

Complete text:	King Michael was a popular leader, a man whom people trusted.
Quotation:	The author writes that "King Michael was a man whom people trusted."

- Use quotation marks to set off titles of *short* works, such as poems, articles, essays, and stories. For *longer* works, such as books, plays, magazines, and newspapers, use underlining.

Short works:	"Dreams" (poem), "How to Get the Most for Your Money" (magazine article), "To Build a Fire" (story)
Longer works:	Invisible Man (book), The Crucible (play), Sports Illustrated (magazine), The Boston Globe (newspaper)

REVIEW

Here is a summary of the strategies you've learned in Part 2. To review any of these in more detail, turn back to the pages indicated.

Reading actively (pages 16-18):

- Get information from the prompt.
- Read the passage more than once.
- Skim the questions in advance.
- Be a careful, thoughtful reader.
- Take time to think about difficult sections.
- Consider the elements of fiction and nonfiction.
- Take notes.

Taking notes (pages 18-20):

- Be brief and clear.
- Include paragraph numbers in your notes.
- Use a loose outline form.
- Make note of ideas and details that relate to questions you're going to have to answer.
- Use shortcuts.
- Highlight notes of special importance.

Answering the multiple-choice questions (pages 23-25):
- Read each question carefully.
- Identify key words in the question that point you toward the correct answer.
- Refer back to the reading passage as often as necessary and use your notes to help you.
- Use the context.
- Read, compare, and consider all the choices. Then pick the best and most complete answer.
- Narrow your search.
- Don't get stuck on a difficult question.
- Answer every question.

Answering the open-response questions (pages 30-35):

- Read each question carefully.
- Identify key words in the question.
- Refer back to the reading passage as often as necessary and use your notes to help you.
- Follow these five steps: (1) Make a plan; (2) State your main idea(s); (3) Support your idea(s); (4) Re-read what you've written; (5) Proofread your work.

TIP: Always Support Your Ideas

Whether you're writing a two-paragraph response or a five-paragraph essay, always develop and support your ideas with specific and relevant information.

Without supporting details, a writer's ideas carry no weight. Furthermore, unsupported ideas may not be clear to the reader. In general, you will get a higher score by presenting a few ideas and supporting them well than by presenting many unsupported ideas.

PRACTICE

The reading passages and questions that follow will give you a chance to practice the test-taking strategies that you learned in Part 2. You will have further opportunity to apply these strategies in Part 3. In addition, a complete practice test appears at the end of this book.

Reminder: To answer open-response questions, follow these five steps:

1. Make a plan.
2. State your main idea(s).
3. Support your idea(s).
4. Re-read what you've written.
5. Proofread your work.

| **Reading Selection 1** |

The following excerpt is from the introduction to Living with Art, a book that explores the nature, history, and importance of art. Read the excerpt carefully. Then answer the questions that follow.

Living with Art
by Rita Gilbert

1 Enter the world of Henri Matisse. It is a world of color and pattern and beautiful things. A world of lovely women and wonderful indoor spaces. Two boys have a game of checkers at a table draped in a printed cloth; they are the artist's sons. A young woman plays at a piano that seems to float upward on a wall of vividly patterned wallpaper; she is the artist's daughter. In the background are a sculpture and painting displayed against the furnishings of a French gentleman's home. This is Matisse's world.

2 Matisse chose to live with art, and he shows us his world through his own artistic vision. His eye sought the beautiful, the color against color, the pattern on pattern, the lushness of everyday life. He might pose a model in a coat of brilliant scarlet and flowing pink trousers and call her an *odalisque,* a harem woman. He sets her against a background of lush plants, so that she herself seems an exotic plant to be admired for her colors and shapes. She is ordinary life made extraordinary, life made into art.

3 Or, if you prefer, enter the world of Vincent van Gogh. Follow him as he takes up residence in the little yellow house on a street corner in the southern French town of Arles. The artist was so eager to settle in this house that he began sketching it immediately, as soon as the rental was assured. Then he turned the sketches into an important painting, called *Vincent's House at Arles.* Later he made another painting of his bedroom inside the house. Van Gogh chose to live with art, and he spent most of his adult life painting images of his life—his own likeness, his friends, the landscape he inhabited, his house, his special chair. For Van Gogh, *living* and *art* were practically the same thing. This is Van Gogh's world.

4 Relatively few of us will commit a lifetime to art, as Matisse and Van Gogh did, but that doesn't mean we are not involved with art. Who lives with art? You do. Everybody does. It would be impossible *not* to live with art, because art is inextricably connected to human existence. Art has been with us since the earliest cave dwellers made their first steps toward civilization, and will be with us as long as civilized life continues on our planet.

You probably have more art in your life than you realize. If you live in a city or town, artists have designed almost everything in your environment.

The buildings in which you live and work, the furniture inside those buildings, the clothes you wear—all were designed by artists in specialized fields. Very likely the walls of your home are decorated with posters, prints,

5 photographs, maybe original paintings, that you have hung to give personal meaning to your world. Perhaps your school or office building has a large-scale sculpture out front, or a fabric hanging or mural inside.

Whether we know it or not, all of us make choices—every day, every minute—with respect to art. We choose one product over another, one garment over another, one way to walk from place to place, basing our decisions largely on the visual attractiveness of the preferred option.

6 We choose to study and enjoy particular works of art or to ignore them. We choose to plan encounters with art, as in museums and galleries, or not to do so. Some people choose to devote their entire lives to the pursuit of art, thereby acquiring the designation of "artist."

Whatever our degree of involvement with art, we must remember that it is a choice. We can go through life like sleepwalkers, ignoring or taking for granted the art around us. Or we can enrich our lives by developing a more

7 active appreciation of the art we live with. This book is about the appreciation of art, which means a combination of understanding and enjoyment. It is possible to heighten our appreciation of art, to learn to see, to take an active interest in the visual world. When we do so, we are only following a basic *aesthetic impulse*—an urge to respond to that which we find beautiful.

Multiple-Choice Questions

1. In paragraph 2, what does the word *exotic* mean?

   A. expensive

   B. strangely beautiful

   C. artificial

   D. tall and thin

2. The author tells readers that

   A. people should commit their lives to art.

   B. art is not as important today as it was in the past.

   C. anyone can be an artist.

   D. art and life are impossible to separate.

3. Which is **not** given in the excerpt as an example of artistic design in our environment?

   A. furniture

   B. buildings

   C. games

   D. clothing

4. The author expresses her belief that

   A. art influences many of our everyday choices.

   B. too many people commit their lives to art.

   C. Matisse and Van Gogh were the only true artists.

   D. modern works of art are overpriced.

5. In the last paragraph, the author suggests that

   A. art should be taken for granted.

   B. a work of art must be truly beautiful to be appreciated.

   C. some people can never learn to appreciate art.

   D. art appreciation requires effort.

6. When the author writes that "we can go through life like sleepwalkers," she is using

   A. a simile.

   B. alliteration.

   C. personification.

   D. a metaphor.

Open-Response Question

7. Using information from the excerpt, explain how art affects our lives.

   _____

   _____

   _____

   _____

   _____

Reading Selection 2

The following selection comes from the opening pages of the novel The Old Man and the Sea by American novelist Ernest Hemingway. Read the excerpt and then answer the questions that follow.

The Old Man and the Sea
by Ernest Hemingway

He was an old man who fished alone in a skiff in the Gulf Stream and he had gone eighty-four days now without taking a fish. In the first forty days a boy had been with him. But after forty days without a fish the boy's parents had told him that the old man was now definitely and finally *salao,* which is the worst form of unlucky, and the boy

1 had gone at their orders in another boat which caught three good fish the first week. It made the boy sad to see the old man come in each day with his skiff empty and he always went down to help him carry either the coiled lines or the gaff and harpoon and the sail that was furled around the mast. The sail was patched with flour sacks and furled, it looked like the flag of permanent defeat.

The old man was thin and gaunt with deep wrinkles in the back of his neck. The brown blotches of the benevolent skin cancer the sun brings from its reflection on the tropic sea were on his cheeks. The blotches ran

2 well down the sides of his face and his hands had the deep-creased scars from handling heavy fish on the cords. But none of these scars were fresh. They were as old as erosions in a fishless desert.

Everything about him was old except his eyes and they were the same

3 color as the sea and were cheerful and undefeated.

"Santiago," the boy said to him as they climbed the bank from where

4 the skiff was hauled up. "I could go with you again. We've made some money."

5 The old man man had taught the boy to fish and the boy loved him.

6 "No," the old man said. "You're with a lucky boat. Stay with them."

"But remember how you went eighty-seven days without fish and then

7 we caught big ones every day for three weeks."

"I remember," the old man said. "I know you did not leave me because

8 you doubted."

9 "It was papa made me leave. I am a boy and I must obey him."

10 "I know, the old man said. "It is quite normal."

11 "He hasn't much faith."

12 "No," the old man said. "But we have. Haven't we?"

13 "Yes," the boy said.

Multiple-Choice Questions

1. Which word is closest to the meaning of *salao* in paragraph 1?

   A. foolish

   B. jinxed

   C. old

   D. stubborn

2. Why did the boy switch to another boat?

   A. His parents made him.

   B. He lost faith in the old man.

   C. He thought he could earn more money.

   D. The other boat was larger.

3. When Hemingway writes that the "sail was patched with flour sacks and, furled, it looked like the flag of permanent defeat," he is using

   A. allegory.

   B. hyperbole.

   C. a simile.

   D. a metaphor.

4. In paragraph 2, Hemingway writes,". . . his hands had the deep-creased scars from handling heavy fish on the cords. But none of these scars were fresh." This suggests that the man

   A. is not a good fisherman.

   B. does not use proper fishing gear.

   C. was attacked by a large fish.

   D. has been a fisherman for a long time.

5. The boy is the fisherman's

    A. youngest son.

    B. helper and friend.

    C. nephew.

    D. grandson.

6. The old man and the boy agree that

    A. the fisherman's luck will change.

    B. the fisherman should stop fishing.

    C. it's time the old man bought a new boat.

    D. the boy should return to the old man's boat.

Open-Response Question

7. Describe the relationship between the old man and the boy. Use details from the excerpt to support your answer.

_____

_____

_____

_____

_____

_____

P A R T   T H R E E

MCAS Language and Literature: Reading and Thinking Skills

"Reading furnishes the mind only with materials of knowledge; it is thinking makes what we read ours."

The English philosopher John Locke wrote these words 300 years ago. They describe the all-important link between reading and thinking.

This part of the book will help you develop both your reading and thinking skills. When you take the MCAS English Language Arts exam, you'll apply these skills in combination with the test-taking strategies that you learned in Part 2.

The multiple-choice and open-response questions in the Language and Literature portion of the MCAS exam call on a variety of skills. Usually, you'll apply several skills together to answer a question. For example, to answer a question about an author's purpose or point of view, you have to understand the author's key ideas. To grasp these ideas, you may need to make inferences and draw conclusions.

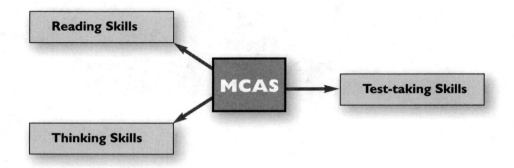

Although the sections of Part 3 focus on individual skills, keep in mind that these skills work together. As you do the activities and answer the practice questions in this part, notice how all reading and thinking skills are interconnected. Notice, too, that you can apply these skills to all kinds of informational and literary selections.

3-1 Identifying Key Ideas and Information

CONCEPTS TO UNDERSTAND

Everything you read has a point. Whether it's a novel or a play, an article or an essay, the author has put words on paper in order to communicate. Your first task as a reader is to understand the author's point: the idea or ideas that the author wants to get across.

Some reading passages on the MCAS exam consist of only a few paragraphs, while others are much longer. Regardless of a selection's length, each paragraph of the selection usually has a *main idea,* and all the main ideas generally relate to the selection's *theme* or *central point.*

Note the words *usually* and *generally* in the previous sentence. Unlike some clothing, there is no "one size fits all" when it comes to reading selections. Literary works are very different from informational works, and every genre has its own unique features. For these reasons, you have to adapt the reading strategies you learn to individual selections.

With that in mind, let's look at some basics.

- The *theme* or *central point* of an informational or literary work is the principal point of the work, the main focus or underlying meaning. The theme or central point is developed through the paragraphs of the work.

In informational works, authors usually state their theme directly or make their meaning clear through the use of supporting information. For example, in an article warning about the dangers of drug use, an author might include facts about the effects of various drugs and statistics about drug-related deaths.

In literary works, authors may also express their theme directly. More commonly, however, they imply their point through characters and events. For example, the author of a short story might imply the theme that *people get what they deserve* by showing evil characters suffering for their deeds.

The theme or central point is also sometimes called a *central idea,* a *controlling idea,* or a *thesis.*

- The *main idea* of a paragraph is the most important point the author makes. The main idea is what the whole paragraph is about.

A paragraph's main idea may or may not be directly stated. A main idea that is not directly stated is called an *implied* main idea.

If the main idea of a paragraph is directly stated, it's usually expressed in a *topic sentence*. However, not all paragraphs have topic sentences. Paragraphs in informational reading passages are more likely to have topic sentences than paragraphs in literary selections.

- Authors develop and support their ideas with *supporting information,* such as facts, details, examples, reasons, statistics, and quotations. The supporting information in a paragraph tells more about the main idea.

Fill in the blanks: Authors of _____

works usually state their theme directly or convey their

meaning through supporting information. Authors of

_____ works are more likely to imply

their theme.

Look at the diagram below. It shows the typical structure of a short informational passage, such as an essay or article. Notice how the parts are interconnected.

PARTS OF A WHOLE
(informational passage)

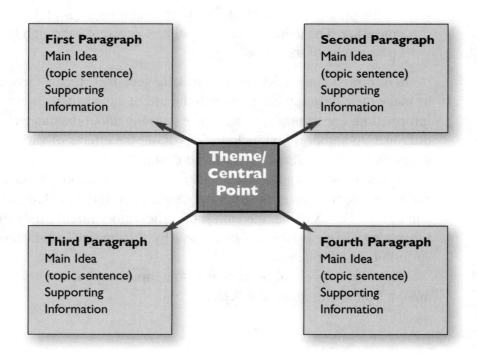

Here's how the diagram might apply to an actual reading passage,
an excerpt from an article titled "Saving and Investing Your Money":

SAVING AND INVESTING YOUR MONEY

First Paragraph

Main idea:
Banks offer the safest means
of saving money, although
depositors won't earn as
high a rate of return as they
might elsewhere.

Supporting information:
The author discusses
savings accounts and
certificates of deposit,
explaining their advantages
and disadvantages.

Third Paragraph

Main idea:
Investing in the stock
market offers the possibility
of high returns, but stocks
are more risky than bonds.

Supporting information:
The author explains what
stocks are and tells why
stock investments can be
very good or very bad.

Theme/Central Point:
There are many ways
to save and invest
money, each having
pros and cons.

Second Paragraph

Main idea:
Bonds are a popular
alternative to bank
accounts, but they are
not without risk.

Supporting information:
The author describes
different types of bonds
and discusses their risks.

Fourth Paragraph

Main idea:
Many people choose mutual
funds because they offer the
possibility of high returns
with less risk than
individual stocks.

Supporting information:
The author explains what
mutual funds are, describes
several types, and discusses
the advantages and
disadvantages of investing
in them.

Activity A: Relating Parts to the Whole

Answer the following question in a short paragraph. Support your answer with specific examples from a selection that you have read for class.

> How are the main ideas of individual paragraphs related to a selection's theme or central point?

_____

_____

_____

READING STRATEGIES:
IDENTIFYING KEY IDEAS AND INFORMATION

To understand the meaning of a reading passage, you need to understand the ideas and information that the author is communicating. The following strategies will help you zero in on the theme/central point of reading selections and the main idea and supporting information in paragraphs.

Keep in mind what you read earlier: Every reading selection is unique. You have to adapt the strategies you learn to individual selections.

How MCAS Exam Questions Are Worded

An important suggestion made in Part 2 was to read each exam question carefully and be sure you understand what the question is asking. Here's one example of why reading questions carefully is so important.

The multiple-choice and open-response questions on the MCAS exam usually do *not* use the terms *theme, central point,* and *main idea.* However, many questions on the exam relate directly or indirectly to the concepts behind these terms. In other words, *you'll often have to identify a central point or main idea even though the question doesn't say so in those words.*

Look at the following questions. Think about how each one relates either to theme/central point or main idea:

What does the author want readers to remember most from this speech?

According to paragraph 3, the primary purpose of education is . . .

The author's account of her childhood shows that . . .

What is the main purpose of this article?

The author expresses his belief that . . .

In the first paragraph, the author suggests that . . .

What lesson do the characters learn?

Questions like these in effect ask you to identify a central point or a main idea, without actually using those terms.

Identifying the Theme/Central Point

To identify the theme or central point of an *informational* reading passage:

- **Think about the title and the introductory prompt**. The title often suggests what the reading passage is about. The prompt provides helpful information about the passage and/or the author.
- **Consider main ideas and supporting information.** Think about how the main ideas are connected and what underlying point they all relate to.

Similarly, consider what supporting information the author has chosen to include, and why. Look for a pattern. Suppose, for example, that an author includes many examples of violence in Saturday morning cartoons. What point might the author be making about children's television?

- **Get a feel for the *whole* selection, not just parts of it.**
  As you read, ask yourself: *What's the point of this selection? What's the author's purpose in writing it?* The answers to these questions will help you find the central point.

Also pay special attention to the beginning and end of a selection. Opening and closing paragraphs often summarize or repeat the central point.

To identify the theme or central point of a *literary* reading passage, you can adapt the same strategies that you would use for an informational passage:

- Think about the title and the prompt.
- Consider main ideas and supporting information.
- Get a feel for the whole selection.

However, because the authors of literary works are more likely to *imply* their ideas, you'll have to rely more on your ability to read between the lines, or *make inferences*. You'll learn about making inferences in section 3-2, *Making Inferences and Drawing Conclusions*. For now, here are several guidelines to help you identify the theme of a literary selection:

- **Think about the characters.** Pay careful attention to their words, thoughts, and actions. Which characters does the author show in a positive light? Which are shown negatively? Why?
- **Think about the story line.** Every event in a novel, short story, or play is carefully planned by the author. Ask yourself why the story unfolds as it does. What is the author suggesting through the events? What conflict is involved? How does the author seem to feel about this conflict?
- **Think about consequences.** What happens as a consequence of characters' actions? What message may the author be sending with these consequences? For example, are honest characters rewarded for their honesty, while deceitful characters are punished?
- **Think about literary elements and techniques.** How does the author use literary elements and techniques to make a point? For example, what events in the story or poem have symbolic meaning? What details reveal how a character feels? You'll read more about literary elements and techniques in section 3-6, *Analyzing Elements of Fiction, Nonfiction, and Poetry*. For tips on reading poetry, review the box on page 17.

Fill in the blank: Authors often summarize or repeat their _____ in the opening or closing paragraph of a selection.

TIP: Analyze Excerpts Just as You Would Whole Works

Most reading selections on the MCAS exam are excerpts, not complete works. This is worth noting because in general a short passage cannot fully convey the theme of a long work such as a novel or play.

Nevertheless, every passage on the exam states or implies important ideas. These ideas usually relate to the theme of the whole work. Furthermore, in some cases, the excerpt has been chosen precisely because it does reveal the work's overall theme.

Identifying the Main Idea of a Paragraph

- **Look for a topic sentence.** The topic sentence—if the paragraph has one—states the main idea. It's often the first sentence in a paragraph, but it may also appear in the middle of a paragraph or at the end.
- **Study the paragraph.** Ask yourself: *What's the whole paragraph about? What point is the author making?*

If the main idea is implied rather than stated, you can figure it out by carefully examining the supporting information. The facts, details, and examples will guide you toward the main idea. Think about what they have in common, how they all fit together. Try to summarize the point of the paragraph in your own words.

- **Consider how the part fits into the whole.** Together, the paragraphs of a selection support and develop a central point. You can use this fact to help you figure out what a paragraph is about. For example, if the first three paragraphs of a selection all describe the horrors of war, it's likely that the fourth paragraph, too, will deal with that theme.
- **Look for signal words.** Certain phrases call attention to main ideas. Here are a few examples:

Words That May Signal Main Ideas

the single most important	the main reason that
the greatest problem	most of all
the chief result	above all

Identifying Supporting Information

- **Think about the main idea.** In much the same way that supporting information guides you toward a paragraph's main idea, the main idea can point you toward important information. For example, if a paragraph begins with a topic sentence stating the main idea, you can look for specific facts, details, and other information that supports that idea.
- **Use the 5 W's + H.** Journalists try to answer six questions when they gather information. These questions are sometimes referred to as the 5 W's + H:

    Who?   When?

    What?   Why?

    Where?   How?

You can ask yourself these same questions to identify important supporting information. Although not every paragraph will contain the answers to all six questions, the questions you can answer will highlight key points.

TIP: Distinguish Between Facts and Opinions

Authors use facts to develop and support their ideas. However, they often mix facts with opinions. Think critically about what you read, so that you can tell one from the other. To learn about distinguishing fact from opinion, read the box on page 134.

APPLY YOUR KNOWLEDGE

- The following selection is an excerpt from a book about marine science, the study of the sea and sea life. Read the passage and answer the questions. Use the reading strategies that you've learned.
- After you have finished, read the *Think It Through* that follows to see how one student answered the questions.

Marine Animals at Risk

1   The great auk *(Pinguinus impennis)* was last seen alive in 1844. This marine bird stood about 60 centimeters tall and looked like it was part duck and part penguin. Although it was once abundant along the North Atlantic coast, the great auk will not be seen again because it is extinct.

2   When a species become *extinct*, it no longer exists anywhere in the world. How did the great auk become extinct? Great auks inhabited the shallow coastal waters near Newfoundland, Canada. Although fast-swimming while in pursuit of fish, on land these seabirds were flightless, awkward, and easy prey for hungry sailors. As a result, by the mid-1850s the great auks were exterminated hunted into extinction.

3   Since the 1600s, when European settlers first came to America, more than 500 animal species have become extinct. More than three times that many are now in danger of extinction in America. Some of these species are marine animals. Table 23-2 lists a few seabirds and marine mammals that already have become extinct as a result human activities within the past 200 years.

4   Unfortunately, the extinction of animal species continues. An example of a marine animal found in American waters that is threatened with extinction is the Florida (or West Indian) manatee. The manatee inhabits the rivers and waterways along Florida's Gulf and Atlantic coasts (and the Caribbean Sea). During the winter, these mammals move into warm coastal rivers and graze on vegetation. As summer approaches and the ocean warms, the manatees leave the protection of the inland rivers and migrate along the coast. Many manatees get struck by power boats and are injured or killed by the boat propellers. It is thought that some die from poisoning by red tide microorganisms. The rapid development along Florida's coast also has contributed to a decline in the manatee population, mainly due to a loss of habitat.

TABLE 23-2. RECENTLY EXTINCT MARINE BIRDS AND MAMMALS

Species	Date Last Seen	Habitat
Stellar's sea cow	1768	Aleutian Islands
Great auk	1844	No. Atlantic Coast
Labrador duck	1875	No. Atlantic Coast
Sea mink	1880	Coast of Maine
Caribbean monk seal	1962	Caribbean Sea
Dusky seaside sparrow	1987	Atlantic Coast

1. What is the most important point that the author makes in this excerpt? Give reasons to support your answer.

_____

_____

_____

2. According to paragraph 2, what happened to the great auk?

_____

_____

_____

_____

3. What is the main idea of paragraph 4?

_____

_____

_____

4. What supporting information does the author use to develop the main idea of paragraph 4?

_____

_____

_____

5. How do paragraphs 3 and 4 relate to the central point?

_____

_____

_____

Think It Through

1. What is the most important point that the author makes in this excerpt? Give reasons to support your answer.

    This question asks me to identify the most important, or central, point of the excerpt. The author's most important point is that marine animals and other animal species are in danger of extinction. I came to this conclusion for several reasons.

    First, the title suggests the idea of animals in danger. Second, the supporting information in all of the paragraphs relates to the idea of extinction, either in the past or the present. Third, paragraph 3 clearly emphasizes the danger of extinction.

2. According to paragraph 2, what happened to the great auk?

    This question is really asking me to identify the main idea of paragraph 2. That is: sailors hunted the great auk into extinction. Although the paragraph doesn't have a clear topic sentence, all the supporting information points to this main idea.

3. What is the main idea of paragraph 4?

    The main idea is stated in a topic sentence: "Unfortunately, the extinction of animal species continues."

4. What supporting information does the author use to develop the main idea of paragraph 4?

    The author develops the main idea by giving an example of an animal that is presently in danger, the manatee. The author describes in detail why the manatee is threatened.

5. How do paragraphs 3 and 4 relate to the central point?

> The central point is that marine animals and other species are
> in danger of extinction. Paragraph 3 explains that hundreds of
> species have already become extinct and many more are now in
> danger. Paragraph 4 gives a detailed example of the ongoing
> process of extinction.

APPLY YOUR KNOWLEDGE

- The following selection is an excerpt from a short story called "The Apprentice." Read the passage and answer the questions. Use the reading strategies that you've learned.
- After you have finished, read the *Think It Through* that follows to see how one student answered the questions.

The Apprentice
by Dorothy Canfield Fisher

1 The day had been one of the unbearable ones, when every sound had set her teeth on edge like chalk creaking on a blackboard, when every word her father or mother said to her or did not say to her seemed an intentional injustice. And of course it would happen, as the fitting end to such a day, that just as the sun went down back of the mountain and the long twilight began, she noticed that *Rollie was not around.

2 Tense with exasperation at what her mother would say, she began to call him in a carefully casual tone—she would simply explode if mother got going: "Here Rollie! He-ere boy! Want to go for a walk, Rollie?" Whistling to him cheerfully, her heart full of wrath at the way the world treated her, she made the rounds of his haunts: the corner of the woodshed, where he liked to curl up on the wool of father's discarded old sweater; the hay barn, the cow barn, the sunny spot on the side porch. No Rollie.

3 Perhaps he had sneaked upstairs to lie on her bed, where he was not supposed to go—not that *she* would have minded! That rule was a part of mother's fussiness, part, too, of mother's bossiness. It was *her* bed, wasn't it? But was she allowed the say-so about it? Not on your life. They *said* she could have things the way she wanted in her own room, now she was in her teens, but—her heart burned at unfairness as she took the stairs stormily, two steps at a time, her pigtails flopping up and down on her back. If Rollie was there, she was just going to let him stay there, and mother could say what she wanted to.

* Rollie is the girl's pet collie.

1. What is the main idea of paragraph 1?

    _____

    _____

    _____

2. How does supporting information help to convey the main idea
    of paragraph 2?

    _____

    _____

    _____

    _____

3. What does paragraph 3 show about how the girl feels?

    _____

    _____

    _____

    _____

4. What theme does the reading passage suggest? Give reasons for
    your answer.

    _____

    _____

    _____

Think It Through

1. What is the main idea of paragraph 1?

    The main idea is expressed in the first sentence: the girl has had
    an "unbearable" day, when everything has irritated her.

2. How does supporting information help to convey the main idea of paragraph 2?

> The main idea is that the girl is looking for Rollie but can't find the dog. Supporting information makes this idea clear: the girl calls to the dog, whistles to him, and looks for him in all his favorite places, but, "No Rollie."

3. What does paragraph 3 show about how the girl feels?

> Several descriptive details show that the girl feels frustrated and is annoyed with her parents. For example, the author writes that "her heart burned at unfairness as she took the stairs stormily."

4. What theme does the reading passage suggest? Give reasons for your answer.

> The theme of the passage is that the girl is upset with her parents because she feels they treat her unfairly. This theme comes through in all three paragraphs. For example, paragraph 1 says that "every word her father or mother said . . . seemed an intentional injustice." Paragraph 2 describes "her heart full of wrath at the way the world treated her." And in paragraph 3, the girl complains that she can't "have things the way she wanted in her own room."

Activity B: Working with Different Kinds of Passages

You've applied the reading strategies you learned first to an informational selection ("Marine Animals at Risk") and then to a literary selection ("The Apprentice"). Based on your experience, answer the following questions.

1. What differences did you find in terms of identifying ideas and supporting details in informational and literary selections? Did you find one kind of selection easier to work with than the other? If so, why?

_____

_____

_____

2. What tips can you offer other students for zeroing in on the meaning of different kinds of reading passages?

_____

_____

_____

3. Share and compare your answers to the preceding questions with the answers of other students. What tips from other students did you find helpful?

_____

_____

_____

REVIEW

Here is a brief summary of what you've learned in section 3-1. To review concepts or strategies in more detail, turn back to the pages indicated.

Concepts to Understand (pages 55-58):

- The *theme* or *central point* is the principal point of a work, the main focus or underlying meaning.
- The *main idea* of a paragraph is the most important point the author makes. The main idea is what the whole paragraph is about. It may be directly stated or implied.
- Authors develop their ideas with *supporting information,* such as facts, details, and examples.

Identifying the theme/central point (pages 59-61):

any selection
- Think about the title and the introductory prompt.
- Consider main ideas and supporting information.
- Get a feel for the whole selection, not just parts of it.

literary selections
- Think about the characters.
- Think about the story line.
- Think about consequences.
- Think about literary elements and techniques.

Identifying the main idea of a paragraph (page 61):

- Look for a topic sentence.
- Study the paragraph.
- Consider how the part fits into the whole.
- Look for signal words.

Identifying supporting information (page 62):

- Think about the main idea.
- Use the 5 W's + H.

TIP: Base Your Answers on What You Read

Some reading selections on the MCAS exam may deal with subjects that you are familiar with. You might even encounter an excerpt from a book that you've read. Don't be distracted by what you already know about a particular subject or selection. Base your answers to questions on the ideas and information that are in a given reading passage.

PRACTICE

The selections and questions that follow will give you a chance to practice the reading strategies that you've learned in Part 3 and the test-taking strategies that you learned in Part 2. Because MCAS exam questions call for a combination of skills, practice questions touch on skills beyond those covered in just this section.

Reminder: *Although MCAS exam questions generally don't use the terms* theme, central point, *and* main idea, *many questions relate to the concepts behind these terms. In other words, you'll often have to identify—or infer—a central point or main idea even though the question doesn't say so in those words.*

Reading Selection 1

Bertrand Russell was a 20th century British philosopher and mathematician. In this brief essay, he talks about his life's passions. Read the essay carefully. Then answer the questions that follow.

What I Have Lived For

by Bertrand Russell

1   Three passions, simple but overwhelmingly strong, have governed my life; the longing for love, the search for knowledge, and unbearable pity for the suffering of mankind. These passions, like great winds, have blown me hither and thither, in a wayward course, over a deep ocean of anguish, reaching to the very verge of despair.

2   I have sought love, first, because it brings ecstasy—ecstasy so great that I would often have sacrificed all the rest of life for a few hours of this joy. I have sought it, next, because it relieves loneliness—that terrible loneliness in which one shivering consciousness looks over the rim of the world into the cold unfathomable lifeless abyss. I have sought it, finally, because in the union of love I have seen, in a mystic miniature, the prefiguring vision of the heaven that saints and poets have imagined. This is what I sought, and though it might seem too good for human life, this is what—at last—I have found.

3   With equal passion I have sought knowledge. I have wished to understand the hearts of men. I have wished to know why the stars shine. And I have tried to apprehend the Pythagorean power by which number holds sway above the flux. A little of this, but not much, I have achieved.

4   Love and knowledge, so far as they were possible, led upward toward the heavens. But always pity brought me back to earth. Echoes of cries of pain reverberate in my heart. Children in famine, victims tortured by oppressors, helpless old people a hated burden to their sons, and the whole world of loneliness, poverty, and pain make a mockery of what human life should be. I long to alleviate the evil, but I cannot, and I too suffer.

5   This has been my life. I have found it worth living, and would gladly live it again if the chance were offered me.

Multiple-Choice Questions

1. In this essay, which does Russell **not** include as one of the passions of his life?

   A. the quest for knowledge

   B. the search for love

   C. the pursuit of fame

   D. pity for people who suffer

2. What was the **strongest** reason for which Russell pursued love?

   A. Love suggested to him a vision of heaven.

   B. Love made him less afraid of death.

   C. Love brought him intense joy.

   D. Love made him feel less lonely.

3. In paragraph 4, the author expresses

   A. his deep love of knowledge.

   B. frustration at being unable to help those in need.

   C. his dislike of human life.

   D. his views about political oppression.

4. Looking back on his life, Russell is

   A. filled with despair.

   B. angry at those who caused him pain.

   C. ashamed of how little he has learned.

   D. satisfied with how he has lived.

Open-Response Question

5. Russell writes: "These passions, like great winds, have blown me hither and thither, in a wayward course, over a deep ocean of anguish, reaching to the very verge of despair." What do you think he means by this statement? Use specific information from the essay to support your answer.

_____

_____

_____

_____

_____

This modern retelling of an ancient legend has an important lesson to teach. Read the story and then answer the questions that follow.

The Sword of Damocles

1   There once was a king named Dionysius who ruled in Syracuse, the richest city in Sicily. He lived in a fine palace where there were many beautiful and costly things, and he was waited upon by a host of servants who were always ready to do his bidding.

2   Naturally, because Dionysius had so much wealth and power, there were many in Syracuse who envied his good fortune. Damocles was one of these. He was one of Dionysius's best friends, and he was always saying to him, "How lucky you are! You have everything anyone could wish for. You must be the happiest man in the world."

3   One day Dionysius grew tired of hearing such talk. "Come now," he said, "do you really think I'm happier than everyone else?"

4   "But of course you are," Damocles replied. "Look at the great treasures you possess and the power you hold. You have not a single worry in the world. How could life be any better?"

5   "Perhaps you would like to change places with me," said Dionysius.

6   "Oh, I would never dream of that," said Damocles. "But if I could only have your riches and your pleasures for one day, I should never want any greater happiness."

7   "Very well. Trade places with me for just one day, and you shall have them."

8   And so, the next day, Damocles was led to the palace, and all the servants were instructed to treat him as their master. They dressed him in royal robes and placed on his head a crown of gold. He sat down at a table in the banquet hall, and rich foods were set before him. Nothing was wanting that could give him pleasure. There were costly wines, and beautiful flowers, and rare perfumes, and delightful music. He rested himself among soft cushions and felt he was the happiest man in all the world.

9   "Ah, this is the life, he signed to Dionysius, who sat at the other end of the long table. "I've never enjoyed myself so much."

10 And as he raised a cup to his lips, he lifted his eyes toward the ceiling. What was that dangling above him, with its point almost touching his head?

11 Damocles stiffened. The smile faded from his lips, and his face turned ashy pale. His hands trembled. He wanted no more food, no more wine, no more music. He only wanted to be out of the palace, far away, he cared not where. For directly above his head hung a sword, held to the ceiling by only a single horsehair. Its sharp blade glittered as it pointed right between his eyes. He started to jump up and run, but stopped himself, frightened that any sudden move might snap the thing thread and bring the sword down. He sat frozen to his chair.

12   "What is the matter, my friend?" Dionysius asked. "You seem to have lost your appetite."

13   "That sword! That sword!" whispered Damocles. "Don't you see it?"

14   "Of course I see it," said Dionysius. "I see it every day. It always hangs over my head, and there is always the chance someone or something may cut the slim thread. Perhaps one of my own advisors will grow jealous of my power and try to kill me. Or someone may spread lies about me, to turn the people against me. It may be that a neighboring kingdom will send an army to seize this throne. Or I might make an unwise decision that will bring my downfall. If you want to be a leader, you must be willing to accept these risks. They come with the power, you see."

15   "Yes, I do see," said Damocles. "I see now that I was mistaken, and that you have much to think about besides your riches and fame. Please take your place, and let me go back to my own house."

16   And as long as he lived, Damocles never again wanted to change places, even for a moment, with the king.

Multiple-Choice Questions

1. At first, Damocles believes that

    A. he has a better life than Dionysius.

    B. he would make a better king than Dionysius.

    C. Dionysius lives in constant danger.

    D. Dionysius is the most fortunate of all men.

2. In paragraph 11, Damocles' "smile faded from his lips, and his face turned ashy pale." Why does this happen?

    A. Dionysius threatens Damocles with a sword.

    B. Damocles sees a sword above his head, hanging by a hair.

    C. Damocles has consumed too much food and wine.

    D. Damocles fears that he has offended the king.

3. The sword in this story can be seen as a symbol for

    A. a ruler's need to protect oneself.

    B. the power of a strong leader.

    C. the danger that is part of a king's life.

    D. courage and strength.

4. After his experience trading places with Dionysius, Damocles

    A. no longer feels envious of the king.

    B. wants more than ever to be the king.

    C. decides that Dionysius is a foolish ruler.

    D. feels much the same as he did before.

5. The lesson taught by this story can best be stated as

    A. the end does not justify the means.

    B. with power comes risk.

    C. few people have the wisdom to be king.

    D. nothing ventured, nothing gained.

Open-Response Question

6. Instead of just explaining matters to his friend, Dionysius chose a different way to get his point across. Was Dionysius's approach effective? Support your answer with details from the story.

_____

_____

_____

_____

_____

_____

3-2 Making Inferences and Drawing Conclusions

CONCEPTS TO UNDERSTAND

When you read a selection, your mind takes in information and combines it with knowledge that you already have. This process of combining what you read with what you know helps you understand the meaning of the selection. Let's look more closely at a key part of the process, *making inferences.*

- To *infer* means to combine information you read with your own knowledge, experience, and judgment to make an educated guess. When you make an inference, you reach an understanding or draw a conclusion that goes beyond what is directly stated. Your inference helps you figure out an author's implied ideas.

Think about the following brief excerpts:

Rebecca heard a loud thunk. *The car pulled sharply to the left. She had to grip the steering wheel tightly to keep the car on the road.*

What happened? How do you know?

Inference/conclusion: The car Rebecca is driving had a flat tire. Based on your knowledge and judgment, you can figure this out from the details given, even though the author does not specifically mention the tire.

The sky darkened, and a sudden wind slashed through the trees. Jake heard a distant rumble. He hurried home.

Why did Jake hurry home? How do you know?

Inference/conclusion: From your knowledge and experience, you can infer that a thunderstorm is approaching. You can also conclude that Jake is rushing to avoid the storm.

Authors of fiction and poetry typically show their meaning rather than state it. Look at this excerpt:

Kaitlyn tore open the envelope. Her hands were trembling. She held her breath as she read the letter once, then a second time. Her face relaxed into a broad grin. "Yes!" she gasped, clutching the paper as though it might disappear if she didn't hold it tightly enough.

How did Kaitlyn feel before opening the envelope? How did she feel after reading the letter? How do you know?

Inference/conclusion: You can infer Kaitlyn's feelings from the details. For example, you know that trembling hands and holding one's breath are signs of nervousness. After reading the letter, Kaitlyn's "face relaxed into a broad grin"—suggesting feelings of relief and happiness.

Ideas and information from reading	+	Your knowledge and experience	→	Make inferences and draw conclusions

- You can make inferences about many different aspects of what you read. For example, when you read a literary selection, you may make inferences about the theme, about characters' actions and feelings, or about events that take place. When you read an informational selection, you may make inferences about the central point, about implied ideas in paragraphs, or about the author's attitude.
- You make inferences on the basis of facts, details, examples, and other information. It's often possible to make more than one inference or draw more than one conclusion from given information. You have to use your judgment to make the inference that seems most reasonable. Here's an example:

The salesman rang Mrs. Steger's doorbell, but she did not come to the door.

Inference/conclusion:
Mrs. Steger is not home.
 or
Mrs. Steger is home, but she does not want to come to the door.
 or
Mrs. Steger is home, but she is unable to come to the door.

Fill in the blank: Making inferences helps you figure out an author's _____ ideas.

TIP: Ponder the Clues

Making inferences is a lot like doing detective work. First, you have to find the "clues." Then you have to figure out what they mean. And just as detectives take time to think things through, you too need to carefully evaluate all the "evidence" before reaching a conclusion.

Activity C: Inferring Information

Making inferences isn't just a reading skill. You infer information every day without even realizing it. For example, if you see people laughing as they leave a theater, you infer that they enjoyed the movie. If there are no lights on in a store, you conclude that the store is closed.

Work with a partner. List three inferences that you've made in daily life, and tell what information helped you make each one.

1. Inference:

   _____

   _____

   _____

   Information:

   _____

   _____

   _____

2. Inference:

_____

_____

_____

Information:

_____

_____

_____

3. Inference:

_____

_____

_____

Information:

_____

_____

_____

READING STRATEGIES: MAKING INFERENCES AND DRAWING CONCLUSIONS

The strategies below will help you make inferences and draw conclusions when you read. Keep in mind that most selections contain stated as well as implied ideas. To fully understand the meaning of a selection, you need to look for both.

- **Put the pieces together.** Think about how ideas and supporting information all fit together. In this way, making inferences is like assembling a jigsaw puzzle. You have to join the pieces to see the whole picture. This "picture" may be the implied main idea of one paragraph or the theme of an entire selection.

- **Pay attention to details.** Lawyers build a case from pieces of information. So do authors. The supporting facts, details, and examples in a selection will point to the idea that the author is communicating. For example, if a character in a novel lives in a huge house and drives an expensive car, what might you infer about the character?

- **Think about connections between events.** What happened first? What happened next? Did one event cause, or result from, another? What event would you expect to happen next? Suppose, for example, that a man is drinking at a party. Later that evening, the man drives his car into a tree. What might you infer about the cause of the crash?

- **Look for comparisons.** To make a point, an author may show how people or things are similar or different, or how they have changed. For instance, suppose an author describes how a journey that took months a century ago takes only hours today. What point might the author be making? You'll learn more about comparisons in section 3-7, *Understanding Comparison and Contrast.*

- **Think about the author's choice of words.** Authors communicate meaning and reveal their point of view (see section 3-5, *Understanding an Author's Purpose and Point of View*) through the specific words they use. For example, compare the following sentences. How did changing two words affect the meaning of the sentence?

    In-line skating is an *exciting* and *challenging* sport.
    In-line skating is a *nerve-racking* and *difficult* sport.

    Answer in your own words: Why do you think that making inferences is sometimes called "reading between the lines"?

    _____

    _____

    _____

    _____

    _____

Activity D: Considering Word Choices

The words that an author chooses may give a positive or negative impression.

1. Next to each word below, write *P* if you think the word conveys a positive image, *N* if you think it gives a negative slant, or *X* if you think the word is neutral or could be *positive* or *negative*. Check a dictionary if you're not sure of a word's meaning.

reckless	_____	arrogant	_____
imaginative	_____	naïve	_____
resourceful	_____	insidious	_____
unique	_____	picturesque	_____
shrewd	_____	elegant	_____
scrawny	_____	affluent	_____
charitable	_____	impetuous	_____

2. Compare your answers with those of another student. Which words did you *not* agree on? Discuss your reasons, and try to agree on one answer.

TIP: Confirm Your Inferences

When you make an inference, look for additional information that confirms—or changes—your inference. This is especially important with literary selections, where new information emerges as the plot develops.

For example, suppose the character in a story gets fired from his job. You infer from the details that he was fired for stealing. However, the last paragraph of the selection suggests that someone else was the real thief. In this case, you have to change your conclusion on the basis of new information.

APPLY YOUR KNOWLEDGE

- The following selection is an excerpt from a book about the history of early civilizations. Read the passage and answer the questions. Use the reading strategies that you've learned.
- After you have finished, read the *Think It Through* that follows to see how one student answered the questions.

Sound Minds in Healthy Bodies

1 The Greeks, especially the Athenians, believed that citizens could not develop their full potential without education. This was a new idea, for earlier peoples had reserved education for priests and rulers. Of course, "citizens" in Greece meant males only, for women were excluded from all political activity. Young girls learned household management from their mothers, and—like them—were expected to stay at home.

2 Athenian boys started school around the age of six, studying arithmetic, music, literature, and writing. They practiced their Greek letters on wax tablets, which could be easily erased. Everyone learned Homer, as much a classic for Greek pupils as Shakespeare is for English-speaking students today.

3 At least as necessary as intellectual learning was physical education. For the Greeks felt that a man attained harmony only when his mind and body were both well developed. Sports included racing, jumping, wrestling, throwing the discus or javelin, and boxing. Even for men who were finished with schooling, the gymnasium was an important place. Here they not only exercised, but also met to discuss business and politics.

4 So important was physical fitness that the Greeks paid tribute to their gods with athletic contests. The Olympic Games, held on the plains of Olympia in the Peloponnesus, honored Zeus. The first recorded games were held in 776 B.C. The Greeks dated their history in terms of the Olympic contests, which occurred every four years. Winners received only a laurel wreath, but were much honored by their communities.

1. What can you conclude from this excerpt about how the ancient Greeks viewed males and females? How do you know?

_____

_____

_____

2. What can you infer from paragraph 1 about how "earlier peoples" regarded the need for education? How do you know?

_____

_____

_____

3. What is the main idea of paragraph 3? How does the author convey this idea?

_____

_____

_____

4. Based on the excerpt, what kind of person do you think the Greeks would consider to be a well-rounded individual? Explain your answer.

_____

_____

_____

Think It Through

1. What can you conclude from this excerpt about how the ancient Greeks viewed males and females? How do you know?

    The ancient Greeks favored males over females. Paragraph 1 says that only males could be citizens and that "women were excluded from all political activity." Girls were "expected to stay at home" like their mothers. I also notice that in paragraph 3, the author refers only to males.

2. What can you infer from paragraph 1 about how "earlier peoples" regarded the need for education? How do you know?

> I can infer that before the Greeks, education for all was not a
>
> generally accepted idea. I know this because the author says
>
> that education had been "reserved . . . for priests and rulers."

3. What is the main idea of paragraph 3? How does the author convey this idea?

> The author conveys the main idea in a topic sentence: At least
>
> as necessary as intellectual learning was physical education.
>
> The two sentences that follow the topic sentence support and
>
> develop this idea.

4. Based on the excerpt, what kind of person do you think the Greeks would consider to be a well-rounded individual? Explain your answer.

> I can conclude from the excerpt that the Greeks would consider
>
> a person (a man) to be well-rounded if he was well-educated and
>
> physically fit. As the author writes, "a man attained harmony
>
> only when his mind and body were both well developed."

APPLY YOUR KNOWLEDGE

- The following selection is an excerpt from a short story. Read the passage and answer the questions. Use the reading strategies that you've learned.
- After you have finished, read the *Think It Through* that follows to see how one student answered the questions.

The Problem with Teenagers

1   "**D**ad, can you give me a lift over to Ben's house?" Adam asked. It was Saturday morning, and the Clark family was finishing breakfast.

     "You know," Mr. Clark said, "when I was your age, I had to

2   walk everywhere."

     "I know, Dad," Adam sighed. He always sighed when his father began

3   with, *When I was your age.* "But he lives all the way over on—"

     "Some of my buddies lived three miles away," Mr. Clark continued.

4   "We used to take turns hiking over to each other's places. Sometimes we'd meet halfway."

     Mrs. Clark smiled but kept silent. She carried several plates to the

5   kitchen sink.

     "So can you, Dad?" Adam persisted. "It's almost nine-thirty. Can you

6   drive me over?"

     "I didn't even have a decent bike," Mr. Clark said. "I had to get by with a piece of junk that I got at a garage sale for five bucks. You've got that

7   mountain bike we bought you last year. What I would have given for a bike like that . . ."

8   "It's raining, Dad. You want me to bike across town in the rain?"

     "It's *drizzling,*" Mr. Clark said, finishing his coffee. "When I was your

9   age, I rode in *any* weather."

     "But, Dad, I have to—"

     Mr. Clark rose and brought his cup to the sink. "I remember one time

10   riding to my friend Bobby's house in the *snow.*" He chuckled at the memory. "Not one of my brightest moves. Nearly killed myself."

11   "Sam," Mrs. Clark said, "I can drive him over . . ."

     Mr. Clark grunted. "Nah, that's okay. I'll do it." He turned back toward

12   the table, stopped. Adam's chair was empty.

     "Hey, where'd the kid go?"

     Mrs. Clark smiled. "Maybe he didn't want to hear any more tales of

13   your childhood days," she said.

     Mr. Clark shook his head. "You know, that's the problem with

14   teenagers. They just don't know how to listen."

1. What message about communication does the author send in this excerpt? Explain your answer.

_____

_____

_____

_____

2. How does the ending help to convey this message?

_____

_____

_____

 Think It Through

1. What message about communication does the author send in this excerpt? Explain your answer.

This question is asking me to infer the author's central point. The message that the author sends is that communication requires listening, not just speaking. Mr. Clark and Adam aren't really communicating, because the father isn't really listening to his son. Mr. Clark seems more interested in what he himself has to say.

2. How does the ending help to convey this message?

By the end, the son has given up and left the room. The father's last comment suggests that his son, like other teenagers, doesn't know how to listen. Here the author is using irony. The problem isn't with teenagers. The problem is with someone like Mr. Clark, who seems to view communication as a one-way street.

Activity E: Getting the Point

Read each passage, and answer the questions.

PASSAGE A

1   Although they were twin sisters, their resemblance was purely physical. If I had a problem, I came to Lauren. She would listen patiently, then do whatever she could to help. If I was sad, Lauren could always raise my spirits. If I was happy, she'd share in my happiness. Cindy's main concern in life was, well, Cindy. "I have no time to listen to your little problems," she'd say. "I've got my own problems." If I was feeling low, Cindy usually wouldn't even notice. And when my spirits were high, Cindy would generally resent my happiness.

2   When the two of them were old enough to head off for college, I had very mixed feelings. "Guess you're an only child now," Lauren said, as we walked to the car. "Don't get too spoiled, Princess Pea." That was her nickname for me, after some fairy tale character. I hugged her tightly, trying not to cry but blubbering all the same. When Cindy left the next week, the last thing she said to me was to keep out of her room. I told her that wouldn't be a problem.

1. How is the narrator related to Lauren and Cindy? How do you know?

_____

_____

_____

2. How is the narrator's relationship with Lauren different from her relationship with Cindy? Support your answer with specific details.

_____

_____

_____

3. Which sister—Lauren or Cindy—would be more likely to have many friends? Why?

_____

_____

_____

_____

PASSAGE B

1   Shopping for food a century ago was a very different experience from visiting a modern supermarket or convenience store. A family would travel to the general store, where flour, sugar, and other basic items were sold in wooden barrels, cotton sacks, and stone containers. Today, food products of all sorts are packaged in cardboard boxes, plastic and glass containers, and aluminum cans. Food companies wrap these products in plastic and paper—often multiple layers—to preserve their freshness, to cushion them against damage, and just to make them look attractive to consumers.

2   All this packaging and wrapping ends up in the same place: the garbage. In fact, Americans discard nearly 200 million tons of garbage annually, much of it wrapping and packaging materials. This figure will only increase as the nation's population continues to grow.

3   What can be done with so much garbage? Existing landfills (garbage dumps) are running out of space, and not many new sites are available. Incinerators can burn some of the garbage, but their smoke pollutes the air, and some of the ash produced is toxic. Dumping garbage into the ocean pollutes sea waters.

4   Government officials, environmentalists, and many others discuss and debate various solutions to the garbage problem. Many people urge that new ways be found to recycle and reuse discarded materials. Others insist that additional methods for disposing of garbage must be devised. Still others suggest that the best first step in solving the problem would be for food and other companies to take a more responsible approach to packaging their products.

5   Meanwhile, garbage mounts up, environmental pollution continues, and shoppers continue to fill their carts with elaborately packaged convenience foods.

1. What is the most important point that the author wants to make? Give reasons for your conclusion.

_____

_____

_____

2. In the first paragraph, how does making a comparison help the author convey the paragraph's main idea?

_____

_____

_____

3. What is the implied main idea of the third paragraph? How do you know?

_____

_____

_____

REVIEW

Here is a brief summary of what you've learned in section 3-2. To review concepts or strategies in more detail, turn back to the pages indicated.

Concepts to Understand (pages 77-79):

- To *infer* means to combine what you read with what you know to make an educated guess. Making *inferences* helps you figure out implied ideas.
- It's often possible to draw more than one conclusion from given information. You have to use your judgment to make the most reasonable inference.
- You can make inferences about many different aspects of literary and informational selections.

Making inferences and drawing conclusions (pages 80-81):

- Put the pieces together.
- Pay attention to details.
- Think about connections between events.
- Look for comparisons.
- Think about the author's choice of words.

PRACTICE

The selections and questions that follow will give you a chance to practice the reading strategies that you've learned in Part 3 *and* the test-taking strategies that you learned in Part 2. Because MCAS exam questions call for a combination of skills, practice questions touch on skills beyond those covered in just this section.

Reminder: Although MCAS exam questions generally don't use the terms *theme, central point,* and *main idea,* many questions relate to the concepts behind these terms. In other words, you'll often have to identify a central point or main idea even though the question doesn't say so in those words.

Reading Selection 1

In the following newspaper column, the author shares with readers a painful but important lesson that he learned a long time ago. Read the column carefully. Then answer the questions that follow.

Bird Girl

by Clark DeLeon

1   There was a weird girl in my high school whom we all called the Bird. We called her that because of her nervous, birdlike movements and the way she would hunch her shoulders toward her ears as if she was hoping her head would disappear into her body. She had sallow skin that looked as if it had never felt the sun, and there was usually a blotchy red rash in the middle of her forehead. She had fine black hair on her arms long enough to comb, and she wore clothes that had been out of fashion since Shirley Temple was singing "The Good Ship Lollipop." She was also the object of such contempt and scorn, such cruel ridicule, that it shames me to this day to think I was part of it, even tacitly.

2   Oh, I was never one to say anything to her face. I wasn't that brave. I'd wait until she hurried by with her books held tightly to her chest and join in the chorus of birdcalls with the other guys. She was always good for a laugh. And it's important when you're a teenager to join the laughter, lest the laughter turn on you.

3   I remember one day when the Bird was surrounded by three or four suburban-variety greasers who had stopped her in the corridor between classes. They were flapping their arms and screeching in her ear. She was terrified. Her eyes darted in panic. A couple of her books fell to the floor. When she stooped to pick them up, they bent over her in a circle, closing in, screeching, screeching.

4   Then this girl came out of nowhere. I'd never seen such anger in a girl before. She went up to the leader of the tormentors and ripped into him with a hot fury. "Stop it!" she shouted. "Can't you see what you're doing?" The guys backed off, stunned. Then the girl went over to the Bird and put her arm around her shoulder and walked her to class.

5   I thought about the Bird when I read about Nathan Faris, the little boy who shot a classmate and killed himself after being the target of teasing by the kids in his school. I thought of how I had been a part of her misery, how more than 20 years later it still bothers me. But I also think of what I learned that day about decency and bravery, about being a human being, from a girl whose name I don't even know. And I wonder if that one act of defiant kindness may have saved another girl's life.

Multiple-Choice Questions

1. The girl was known as "the Bird" because of her

   A. physical movements.

   B. high-pitched voice.

   C. peculiar clothing.

   D. long neck.

2. Recalling how he acted around the Bird, the author feels

   A. jealous.

   B. proud.

   C. regretful.

   D. amused.

3. When he was in high school, the author

   A. came to the Bird's rescue.

   B. did what his peers did.

   C. left the Bird alone.

   D. encouraged others to pick on the Bird.

4. How does the author view the girl who "came out of nowhere" in paragraph 4?

   A. as a bully

   B. as someone who should have minded her own business

   C. as a victim

   D. as someone who performed a heroic act

5. In paragaph 5, why does the author mention Nathan Faris?

   A. Both the Bird and Nathan Faris picked on other kids.

   B. Nathan Faris and the Bird both reacted with violence.

   C. Nathan Faris went to the same high school.

   D. Both Nathan Faris and the Bird were targets of teasing by their classmates.

6. The author's account suggests that

   A. people should not interfere in matters that don't concern them.

   B. people should help those in need.

   C. teenagers are far more cruel than adults.

   D. people like the Bird get what they deserve.

Open-Response Question

7. How is the author's view of events different now from what it was when he was a teen? Do you think he would act differently now in the same situation? Use specific information from the selection to support your answer.

_____

_____

_____

Reading Selection 2

Read the poem and think about the feelings that the poet expresses. Then answer the questions that follow.

The Courage That My Mother Had
by Edna St. Vincent Millay

The courage that my mother had
Went with her, and is with her still;
Rock from New England quarried;
Now granite in a granite hill.

5   The golden brooch my mother wore
She left behind for me to wear;
I have no thing I treasure more;
Yet, it is something I could spare.

Oh, if instead she'd left to me
10   The thing she took into the grave!—
That courage like a rock, which she
Has no more need of, and I have.

Multiple-Choice Questions

1. The poet's **main** purpose in the first stanza is to

   A. tell where her mother's grave is.

   B. describe her mother's jewelry.

   C. compare her mother's courage to rock.

   D. explain how much she misses her mother.

2. What does the poet mean when she writes, "Yet, it is something I could spare" (line 8)?

   A. She wishes her mother had left her different jewelry.

   B. She does not find the golden brooch attractive.

   C. She already has more jewelry than she needs.

   D. She knows that some things matter more than possessions.

3. The final three words of the poem, ". . . and I have," suggest that the poet

   A. needs courage to face a challenge.

   B. is braver than her mother was.

   C. is angry at her mother.

   D. thinks her mother was selfish.

4. Which of the following does the poem not suggest?

   A. The poet admired her mother.

   B. The poet's mother was a strong woman.

   C. The poet leads a carefree life.

   D. The poet regrets that her mother is gone.

Open-Response Question

5. Poets are able to express many feelings using few words. What feelings does Edna St. Vincent Millay express in this poem? Support your answer with evidence from the poem.

   _____

   _____

   _____

   _____

   _____

3-3 Understanding Cause and Effect

CONCEPTS TO UNDERSTAND

Cause-and-effect relationships play an important part in both informational and literary selections. For example, American history books describe the causes and effects of the Civil War. The works of Shakespeare show how one character's actions can cause tragic consequences. Magazines are filled with articles describing how one event led to or resulted from another. In fact, when you think about it, cause and effect plays some role in almost every selection you read.

Here are some basics you should know about cause-and-effect relationships.

- A *cause* is something that produces an effect or makes something happen. A cause may take many different forms. For example, a cause may be an action, an event, a situation, or a reason.
- An *effect* is a result or consequence brought about by a cause.

Think about the cause-and-effect relationships in the following examples.

A hurricane destroyed the village.

hurricane (cause) ——➤ village destroyed (effect)

The people's dissatisfaction with the government led to a revolution.

people's dissatisfaction (cause) ——➤ revolution (effect)

The patient died as a result of a heart attack.

heart attack (cause) ——➤ patient's death (effect)

Leon studied hard and passed the test.

studying hard (cause) ——➤ passing the test (effect)

The dog's constant barking gave Kim a headache.

dog's barking (cause) ——➤ headache (effect)

Josh was so hungry that he ate three sandwiches.

hunger (cause) ——➤ eating three sandwiches (effect)

Label each of the causes on page 96 as an action, an event, a situation, or a reason. (For some causes, more than one label may be appropriate.)

- Although a single cause may produce a single effect, that's often not the case. A cause may produce one effect or *several* effects. Furthermore, an effect may result from one cause or from a *combination of several* causes. Compare the following examples:

One cause, one effect:

   Because of the heavy snowfall, the roof collapsed.

One cause, two effects:

   Because of the heavy snowfall, the roof collapsed and the family had to be evacuated.

Two causes, one effect:

   Because of the heavy snowfall and high winds, the roof collapsed.

- Authors often use cause and effect as an *organizational* method. For example, an author may state an effect in a topic sentence and then explain the causes in the rest of the paragraph:

   | **Topic sentence/effect:** | *The air in this city is rapidly becoming unbreathable.* |
   | **Supporting details/causes:** | Too many cars
Factory pollution
Power plants |

- Cause-and-effect relationships may be direct or indirect. For example, in a novel one character wrongs another character, who then seeks revenge. In this way, an action or event sets in motion a series of other events. The first event is the cause— direct or indirect—of what happens next.

Similarly, in an autobiography the author may describe how she loses her job and spends months searching for a new one. Finally, she is forced to switch to an entirely new line of work, in which she becomes very successful. In this case, the job loss had various direct and indirect effects on the author's life.

Activity F: Recognizing Causes and Effects

Using any books, newspapers, or magazines of your choice, find an example of each of the following cause-and-effect relationships. Effects may be direct or indirect.

1. One cause, one effect:

_____

_____

_____

2. One cause, two or more effects:

_____

_____

_____

3. Two (or more) causes, one effect:

_____

_____

_____

READING STRATEGIES:
UNDERSTANDING CAUSE AND EFFECT

Use the following strategies to help you understand and identify cause-and-effect relationships in informational and literary selections.

As you study these strategies, keep in mind that *causes and effects may be stated or implied.* In informational works such as essays and articles, they are usually stated. In literary works, though, you often have to *infer* causes. (See section 3-2, *Making Inferences and Drawing Conclusions.*) For example, you may have to infer *why* a character in a story did or said something.

> To find the **CAUSE**, ask **Why did it happen?**

> To find the **EFFECT**, ask **What happened?**

- **Ask yourself: What happened? Why did it happen?** In order to identify a cause-and-effect relationship, ask yourself two questions. First, ask what happened—the effect. Next, ask why it happened—the cause. Review the examples of cause-and-effect relationships on page 96.

- **Watch for signal words.** Certain words often (but not always) signal cause-and-effect relationships. Study the following list and the examples that follow. However, remember that authors do not have to use a signal word in order for there to be a cause-and-effect relationship. (Only one of the examples on page 96 uses a signal word. Can you spot it?)

Words That May Signal Cause and Effect		
cause	effect	because
as a result	since	result in
therefore	thus	consequently
due to	so	so that
if then	reason	nevertheless
why	outcome	this (that) is how
bring about	produce	consequence

Examples:

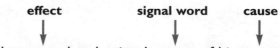

The candidate won the election because of his strong support of equal rights.

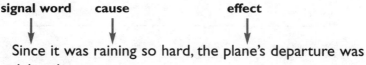

Since it was raining so hard, the plane's departure was delayed.

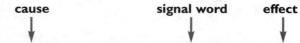

Neither side wanted to compromise. Therefore, the debate continued for hours.

Notice that even though a cause always happens before an effect, the author may state the effect first.

TIP: Watch for Signal Words in Questions

Cause-and-effect signal words sometimes appear in questions on the MCAS exam. Here are a few examples.

Multiple-choice questions:

The narrator traveled to Europe <u>because</u> she . . .

For what <u>reason</u> did the narrator travel to Europe?

Open-response question:

In what ways did the experiment <u>result in</u> unforeseen <u>consequences</u>? Support your answer with . . .

<u>Why</u> did the author's feelings change over the years? Use specific evidence . . .

Activity G: Identifying Causes and Effects

Identify the cause(s) and effect(s) in each of the following.

1. A powerful earthquake struck San Francisco in 1906, starting fires that burned much of the city. More than 2,000 people died.

Cause(s):

_____

_____

_____

_____

Effect(s):

_____

_____

_____

2. Since the colonists found the soil too rocky for farming, they turned to the sea as a food source. In time, fishing and shipbuilding became major industries in the region.

Cause(s):

_____

_____

_____

Effects(s):

_____

_____

_____

3. The furnace quit in the late afternoon, a victim of old age and an uncommonly cold winter. By midnight, the upstairs pipes had frozen and burst. Gushing water poured through the rooms and cascaded down the stairs. By the time Dennis finally arrived home the next day, his once beautiful home resembled a shipwreck.

Cause(s):

_____

_____

_____

Effects:

_____

_____

_____

APPLY YOUR KNOWLEDGE

- Read the following article about global warming and answer the questions. Use the reading strategies that you've learned.
- After you have finished, read the *Think It Through* that follows to see how one student answered the questions.

Will Global Warming Cause a "Meltdown"?

A panel of international scientists is in agreement that the accumulation of heat-trapping gases such as carbon dioxide in the atmosphere—produced by the burning of fossil fuels during the past century—has caused Earth's average daily temperature to increase.

1   Some scientists now fear that this "global warming" will eventually melt the polar ice caps and cause the sea level to rise, resulting in the flooding of coastal regions and small islands.

Recent evidence for a melting of polar ice came from a group of glaciologists (scientists who study glaciers and ice) that works for the British Antarctic Survey, a government organization. Aerial and satellite photos taken of a west Antarctic coastal area during the past 50 years show

2   retreating and shrinkage of several ice shelves. (An ice shelf is a mass of floating ice that is attached to the continent.) In 1995, an 800-square-kilometer chunk of the Larsen Ice Shelf broke up in less than two months. As a result, a 200-kilometer-long series of icebergs were sent floating into the Weddell Sea.

The melting of an ice shelf or icebergs does not increase the total volume of water, so the sea level does not change. However, scientists worry that if melting of the ice shelf continues, this buffer zone between land and sea would disappear, thus exposing the ice sheets and glaciers

3   on land. These glaciers would flow into the sea, where they would melt and cause a rise in sea level. The scientists feel that the ice shelves can be regarded as sensitive indicators of regional climate change.

Some climatologists (scientists who study climate changes) reject the hypothesis that a warming trend will cause a rise in sea level. They argue that a warming trend may actually increase Anatarctic precipitation (in the form of snow). According to this idea, the heavier accumulations of snow that could result would be compressed over time, thereby forming more

4   ice. Other scientists remain neutral. The situation is very complex, so they are not predicting what will happen until they have more information. Meanwhile, leaders of low-lying island nations and coastal areas have expressed great concern for the welfare of their regions.

1. Explain what "global warming" is and why some people are concerned about it.

_____

_____

_____

2. In the last sentence of paragraph 2, what cause-and-effect relationship does the phrase "as a result" signal?

_____

_____

_____

3. According to paragraph 3, what would be the effect of glaciers flowing into the sea?

_____

_____

_____

4. According to paragraph 4, what effects do some climatologists think a warming trend may have?

_____

_____

_____

Think It Through

1. Explain what "global warming" is and why some people are concerned about it.

   "Global warming" refers to "the accumulation of heat-trapping gases . . . in the atmosphere," which causes Earth's temperature to rise. These gases are produced by burning fossil fuels. People are concerned because if the polar ice caps melt, the sea may rise and flood coastal areas and islands.

2. In the last sentence of paragraph 2, what cause-and-effect relationship does the phrase "as a result" signal?

A large chunk of the Larsen Ice Shelf broke up. The result of this breakup was "a 200-kilometer-long series of icebergs . . . floating into the Weddell Sea."

3. According to paragraph 3, what would be the effect of glaciers flowing into the sea?

The glaciers "would melt and cause a rise in sea level."

4. According to paragraph 4, what effects do some climatologists think a warming trend may have?

Some climatologists think that a warming trend may increase Antarctic snowfall. The added snow would eventually be compressed to form more ice.

APPLY YOUR KNOWLEDGE

- The following selection is an excerpt from a short story called "Love! Who'd Have Guessed It?" Read the passage and answer the questions. Use the reading strategies that you've learned.
- After you have finished, read the *Think It Through* that follows to see how one student answered the questions.

Love! Who'd Have Guessed It?
by Cheryl Dale

1   I think skating is the most important thing to me right now. I feel so good knowing that my parents can say, "This is our daughter, Lisa. She's an ice skater." And I am. I'm a good skater, which is why a broken leg was such a blow.

2   I'll never forget that moment it happened. I was walking home from the library at 4 on a Thursday afternoon. The sun was shining and, as usual, I was daydreaming about skating when this kid on a bike came speeding around the corner. Before I ever hit the ground I knew my leg was broken. I heard it snap.

3   I had to spend the night in the hospital, and I remember managing to be really brave until my parents left. Then it hit me—my leg was broken! And, to make matters worse, my cast was pink—bright pink! I guess at some point someone decided plain white was too boring, so they started coloring the mesh in Day-Glo shades so people can see you coming from a mile away! For a person who likes to fade into the woodwork—waking up to find myself practically glowing in the dark was not fun.

4   Finally, I couldn't keep it in any longer. I cried so hard my sobs caused a nurse to show up. She came and patted my hand.

5   Oh, the doctor assured me that I'd be skating again in a couple of months. But I wanted to skate now.

6   I spent the next two weeks sitting home feeling sorry for myself. I couldn't even look at my skates without crying. Finally, I asked Mom to drop me off down at the rink. I thought maybe I'd just watch the others for a while. I hadn't used my crutches much, so I was pretty wobbly, but I managed to get inside. The club members were practicing, so I hobbled over to a rinkside bench and sat down. My legs was hurting from moving it around and the music bringing me close to tears. I was asking myself why I'd come when the coach, Mr. Trent, saw me and came over.

7   "Lisa, how are you doing?" He gave me a hug, which really made me want to cry. Then Karen, another skater, came over. She asked about me too. Before long, several of the kids were gathered around. I didn't even know they knew my name, and here they were wishing me well. That was nice. I even forgot about my leg for a minute.

1. Why did breaking her leg have special significance for Lisa?

   _____

   _____

   _____

2. Paragraph 2 implies that a combination of two factors may have resulted in Lisa being injured. What were they?

   _____

   _____

   _____

3. In the last sentence, Lisa notes that she "even forgot about my leg for a minute." What makes her feel this way?

_____

_____

_____

Think It Through

1. Why did breaking her leg have special significance for Lisa?

   As Lisa explains in the first paragraph, skating is "the most important thing" to her. With a broken leg, she can't skate.

2. Paragraph 2 implies that a combination of two factors may have resulted in Lisa being injured. What were they?

   Lisa admits she was daydreaming when the kid on the bike came around the corner. Maybe if she had been paying more attention, she could have jumped out of the way.

3. In the last sentence, Lisa notes that she "even forgot about my leg for a minute." What makes her feel this way?

   In the last paragraph, Lisa tells how first the coach and then other skaters came over to see how she was and wish her well. This support from other people caused her to forget her troubles, at least for a while.

Activity H: Spotting Signal Words

Cause-and-effect relationships may or may not have signal words. Review the selections on pages 102 and 104-105. Which one uses more signal words? Why do you think this is the case?

_____

_____

_____

REVIEW

Here is a brief summary of what you've learned in section 3-3. To review concepts or strategies in more detail, turn back to the pages indicated.

Concepts to Understand (pages 96-97):

- A *cause* is something that produces an effect or makes something happen. An *effect* is a result or consequence brought about by a cause.
- A cause may produce one effect or several effects.
- An effect may result from one cause or from a combination of causes.
- Cause-and-effect relationships may be stated or implied, direct or indirect.
- Authors often use cause and effect as an organizational method.

Understanding cause and effect (pages 98-100):

- Ask yourself: *What happened? Why did it happen?*
- Watch for signal words.

PRACTICE

The selections and questions that follow will give you a chance to practice the reading strategies that you've learned in Part 3 *and* the test-taking strategies that you learned in Part 2. Because MCAS exam questions call for a combination of skills, practice questions touch on skills beyond those covered in just this section.

Reminder: Selections need not use signal words in order for there to be a cause-and-effect relationship present.

Reading Selection 1

In the following short story, the narrator recalls a significant moment of his childhood. As you read, think about how the narrator felt as child and how he feels now as an adult. When you have finished reading, answer the questions that follow.

Shooting Hoops
by William G. Christ

1
I was somewhere between seven and eight when my dad got it into his head that he wasn't spending enough time with me and my brother after school. Actually, it was probably my mom who had the idea and suggested we needed help. She was an intense woman who dictated the pace of our family's activities. She seemed irritated by what the world dealt her even though her hand looked pretty good from where I was standing. She loved my dad but didn't particularly like Texas, my school, my friends, or my ability to drop food and drink on my clothes no matter how hard I tried to lean over my plate. My dad like my mom was pretty nice though I was always amazed too.

2
One afternoon after school my dad announced he was going to take my brother and me to shoot hoops. My folks had just signed me up for a YMCA basketball league. My dad agreed to take two of my friends along with us. He probably figured that would help me get motivated to exercise. I was an indoor kid who would rather play video games inside and destroy an assortment of making believe beings than play outside and shoot birds with my friend's BB gun. If you were a male Texan, you had to learn to shoot something: gun, pool, hoops.

3
We got to the school where the basketball court, play equipment, and soccer field were located. We shot a couple of hoops to make my dad happy then ran to the playground equipment. My dad followed behind us with the balls. He had brought along a soccer ball figuring if we got tired of hoops he would have a backup sport. I, as usual, complained about having to be there and asked when we would get to go home. My dad looked hurt. My dad tended to be dramatic when it came to trying to

manipulate us. He'd look hurt or happy, at will, hoping that we'd either feel sorry for or want to please him. I can't remember when that technique stopped working, but I think it was before I turned six.

He drifted off with the soccer ball, and my younger brother and one of my friends followed him. My other friend and I started making an alligator in the sand pile by the slide. I liked drawing and sculpture more than bike riding and running. I would look up periodically to find my dad looking
4   my way. In some ways, I think my art inclination appealed to my parents. In some ways, I think my lack of athletic interest troubled them. I could see that my dad was troubled. I called to him to see the great alligator we had created. He said he'd come see it as soon as the game with my younger brother and my friend was over. I think this was his way of punishing me for not being interested in playing soccer with him.

When he finally came over he gave his usual, "That's great," and then said we had to go because the sun was going down. It was then I realized that I was different from my parents. Their desires for me were not my desires for myself. As I stood there and watched my dad walk toward the lot where the car was parked, I was overwhelmed with sadness. Tears
5   welled up in my eyes. The sun, which was setting behind me, threw a warm glow over the schoolyard. It felt like the earth was standing still. As my dad walked away I called to him but he either didn't hear or pretended he didn't hear. He sometimes pretended he didn't hear us when he wanted to stay focused on what he was doing. I called again, but he just kept walking.

Years have gone by since that day in late January. My folks died a couple of years back. I'm sitting here watching my kids playing basketball.
6   Who would have thought that going to shoot hoops could have changed everything? I mark the beginning of my manhood from that day.

Multiple-Choice Questions

1. What causes the conflict between the boy and his father?

    A. The father refuses to play basketball with his son.

    B. The father wants to play only with the boy's younger brother.

    C. The boy prefers soccer to basketball.

    D. The boy has little interest in sports.

2. In paragraph 3, "dad looked hurt" because

    A. he had injured himself playing basketball.

    B. no one wanted to play with him.

    C. his son did not play basketball well.

    D. his son wanted to go home rather than play outdoors.

3. In paragraph 5, why does the narrator feel "overwhelmed with sadness"?

    A. He wants to continue working on his alligator.

    B. He wants to return to the playground.

    C. He has learned a painful lesson.

    D. He is jealous of his brother.

4. What does the narrator mean by the last sentence: "I mark the beginning of my manhood from that day"?

    A. That day, his father began treating him as an adult.

    B. He had come to realize that he was a separate person from his parents.

    C. From that day on, he never played basketball again.

    D. His father's actions had taught him how to be a man.

Open-Response Question

5. In the last paragraph, the narrator asks, "Who would have thought that going to shoot hoops could have changed everything?" What does he mean? Support your answer with specific information from the story.

_____

_____

_____

_____

_____

_____

Reading Selection 2

In this excerpt from a science article, the author describes how infectious diseases (diseases transmitted by viruses or other germs) spread to humans. Read the excerpt carefully. Then answer the questions that follow.

Stirring Up Trouble

by Stephen S. Morse

1   Throughout the history of civilization almost every infectious disease—even nonviral diseases—entered the human population by way of animals. One of the most notorious instances was the black death, a scourge of bubonic plague that may have killed as much as two-thirds of the population of Europe and Asia during two decades in the middle of the fourteenth century. The bacillus that causes plague is harbored by rats—a species long adapted to human settlements—and is transmitted by the fleas they carry. In medieval times, and again in the nineteenth century when a wave of plague swept across China, shipboard rats spread the disease throughout continents and across oceans, leaving social and political turmoil in their wake. A similar disease mechanism, associated with rats, lice, and fleas, generated devastating outbreaks of typhus on European battlegrounds from the sixteenth century through the 1940s.

2   Malaria, persistent tropical killer, also appears to be a by-product of human-induced traffic with animals. The disease, caused by a parasitic protozoan, evidently gained a foothold long ago in western Africa, when slash-and-burn agriculture began to cut into the rainforest. The new clearings offered prime breeding grounds for a species of mosquito, *Anopheles gambiae,* whose preferred bill of fare is human blood. As tropical agriculture spread and clearings became more numerous, *A. gambiae* supplanted mosquito species that were unable to adapt to the new surroundings. In essence, by disrupting the established ecological order, people inadvertently encouraged the adaptation of a "weed" species that more often than not brought them fever and misery.

3   The spread of an equally terrifying tropical disease, yellow fever, was aided by an even more peculiar adaptation. *Aedes aegypti,* the mosquito that carries the yellow fever virus, is highly domesticated: It breeds better in manufactured containers such as cisterns and water casks than in natural bodies of water. This odd affinity allowed. *A. aegypti* to stow away aboard seagoing vessels and cross into the New World with the slave trade. By the middle of the seventeenth century Yellow Jack came to be dreaded among sailors of the tropical Caribbean seas. Because the mosquito that carries yellow fever can survive a voyage of weeks or months, a ship's crew could be ravaged by a chain of on-board epidemics whose cause no one understood. In spite of modern attempts to control the insect, yellow fever remains a major health problem in tropical nations and is still a required immunization for anyone traveling in those regions.

If history teaches one lesson, then, it is that infectious diseases do not arise in a vacuum. Disease-carrying pests have been highly successful at taking advantage of the novel ecological niches—trash heaps, forest clearings, stagnant water sources—opened up by human habitation.

4   Exploration and development too have brought people into contact with isolated reservoirs of illness: Ornithosis, or parrot fever, killed three dozen Americans in 1929 and 1930 when infected tropical birds were imported into the United States. More than any single carrier, it is human encroachment that ultimately precipitates the emergence of killer viruses.

Multiple-Choice Questions

1. According to the article, nearly all infectious diseases

     A. are caused by rats.

     B. originate in the tropical rain forest.

     C. spread to humans by means of animals.

     D. come from the Caribbean.

2. Bubonic plague, the "black death," was spread by

     A. fleas carried by rats.

     B. the bite of a species of mosquito.

     C. the bite of rats.

     D. water stored in certain kinds of containers.

3. Clearing parts of the African rain forest led to

     A. yellow fever epidemics.

     B. increased breeding of the mosquitoes that spread malaria.

     C. typhus outbreaks in Europe.

     D. a decline in the spread of infectious diseases.

4. Which is **not** true about yellow fever?

     A. It is carried by a mosquito.

     B. It no longer poses a threat to people.

     C. The disease took the lives of many sailors.

     D. In the 17th century, no one knew its cause.

5. The article suggests that

   A. insects should be eliminated to stop the spread of diseases.

   B. no disease can be prevented.

   C. scientists don't know very much about how diseases are spread.

   D. people's own actions have led to disease outbreaks.

Open-Response Question

6. How might scientists use their knowledge of how diseases spread to prevent future outbreaks? Use information from the excerpt to support your answer.

   _____

   _____

   _____

   _____

   _____

3-4 Using Context Clues to Determine Meaning

CONCEPTS TO UNDERSTAND

When you're reading a selection, you may come to a word whose meaning is either unfamiliar or unclear to you. For example, a novelist may use a descriptive word that you've never seen before. Or, in an article about medical research, you may encounter a scientific term that is new to you. In such situations, you can use clues from the surrounding context to help you figure out what the word means.

- *Context* refers to the words or sentences that come before and after a particular word.
- You can figure out the meaning of a word by examining its context. The context you need to look at may consist of a few words, the entire sentence, or a paragraph or more.
- A word may have different meanings in different contexts. One meaning may be *literal* (using a word in its usual sense) while another is *figurative* (using a word in an imaginative way to create an effect).

Compare the following examples. What does the word shattered mean in each sentence? How do you know?

> **The baseball shattered the window.** *(literal meaning)*
>
> **The track star shattered all previous records.** *(figurative meaning)*
>
> **Her rejection shattered his self-confidence.** *(figurative meaning)*

- Many words have more than one meaning. You can use context to figure out which meaning applies in a sentence.

For example, the word *condition* may mean "state of health." It may also mean "something that limits or restricts." Which meaning of *condition* applies in the following sentences? How do you know?

> **A long illness had left the woman in a weakened condition.**
>
> **You may go to the party on one condition.**

Answer in your own words: How is the literal meaning of a word different from the figurative meaning?

_____

_____

_____

_____

_____

Activity 1: Understanding Language Through Context

Your knowledge of language can help you infer the meaning of words. Read the poem "Jabberwocky" by Lewis Carroll. How does context help you understand the meaning of the poem's words?

_____

_____

_____

_____

_____

Jabberwocky
Lewis Carroll

'Twas brillig, and the slithy toves
    Did gyre and gimble in the wabe;
All mimsy were the borogoves,
    And the mome raths outgrabe.

5   "Beware the Jabberwock, by son!
      The jaws that bite, the claws that
        catch!
    "Beware the Jubjub bird, and shun
      The frumious Bandersnatch!"

10   He took his vorpal sword in hand:
      Long time the manxome foe he
        sought—

> So rested he by the Tumtum tree,
>   And stood awhile in thought.
>
> 15 And as in uffish though he stood,
>   The Jabberwock, with eyes of
>   flame,
>   Came whiffling through the tulgey
>   wood,
> 20 And burbled as it came!
>
>   One, two! One, two! And through and
>   through
>   The vorpal blade went snicker-snack!
>   He left it dead, and with its head
> 25 He went galumphing back.
>
>   "And hast thou slain the Jabberwock?
>   Come to my arms, my beamish boy!
>   O frabjous day! Callooh! Callay!
>   He chortled in his joy.
>
> 30 'Twas brillig, and the slithy toves
>   Did gyre and gimble in the wabe;
>   All mimsy were the borogoves.
>   And the mome raths outgrabe.

READING STRATEGIES: USING CONTEXT CLUES

The following strategies will help you figure out the meaning of words you don't know. You can use these strategies not only when you take the MCAS exam but *whenever* you are reading.

- **Use the surrounding sentences.** You can often figure out a word by carefully reading and thinking about the rest of the sentence, especially those words nearest the unfamiliar word. However, don't limit yourself to just one sentence. Sometimes you have to look back or ahead several sentences—or even paragraphs—to find context clues.

Example:

Dr. Jessup was the best-known orator in the state. Her powerful words could inspire people to action or move them to tears. People came from miles around to hear her speeches.

An *orator* is someone skilled in public speaking. The second and third sentences provide context clues to the word's meaning.

TIP: For Multiple-Meaning Words, Consider the Selection

For words with more than one meaning, think about the topic and purpose of the selection. One meaning will generally make more sense in a given context than another. For example, the word *operation* has several different meanings. However, in an article about hospitals, it's likely that *operation* would be used to mean a surgical treatment.

- **Look for descriptive information.** Descriptive information may reveal or suggest the meaning of an unfamiliar word.

  Example:

  > *During this turbulent period of history, governments were repeatedly overthrown, and civil wars took countless lives.*

  "Governments were repeatedly overthrown, and civil wars took countless lives" is descriptive information. *Turbulent* means marked by disorder and violence.

- **Look for an explanation.** Authors may explain or define a term the first time they use it.

  Example:

  > *The nature program was run by an ornithologist, an expert in the study of birds.*

  The phrase "an expert in the study of birds" defines *ornithologist.*

- **Look for examples.** Authors may clarify a word's meaning by giving examples.

  Example:

  > *Zeke was an odd man, always speaking in epigrams. "Silence is golden," he would say with a wink. Or "what goes around, comes around."*

  An *epigram* is a short, witty saying. "Silence is golden" and "what goes around, comes around" are examples of epigrams.

- **Look for a synonym.** A *synonym* is a word that means the same or almost the same as another word. A synonym can help you understand the meaning of an unfamiliar word.

  Example:

  > *Ignoring their pleas for mercy, the dictator showed the captured rebels no clemency.*

  Mercy and *clemency* are synonyms.

- **Look for an opposite or contrast.** Authors may reveal a word's meaning by using an opposite or contrasting word or phrase. Contrasts are often, but not always, signaled by such words as *but, not, although, unlike, or.*

  Example:

  > *Unlike his brawny older brother, Jimmy was thin and weak.*

  The word *unlike* signals that the author is contrasting Jimmy and his older brother. *Brawny* means "strong and muscular," in contrast to "thin and weak."

TIP: Put Your Knowledge to Work

In addition to context clues, use your knowledge of language and literature to help you understand word meanings. For example, if you know that bios is Greek for "life," you can figure out such words as biography and biology. If you remember who Narcissus is from Greek mythology, you can figure out the meaning of narcissistic.

APPLY YOUR KNOWLEDGE

- Use the strategies you've learned to figure out the meaning of each underlined word. Write your definition of the word in the space provided. If you're having trouble or you just want to confirm your thinking, check a dictionary.
- After you have finished, read the *Think It Through* that follows to see how one student defined the words.

1. After the jury listened to the victim's <u>version</u> of what happened, they heard the doctor's account.

_____

_____

_____

2. The soldiers advanced cautiously, uncertain if the people of the village were <u>hostile</u> or friendly.

_____

_____

_____

3. Salesmen are the most <u>garrulous</u> creatures on earth. They talk endlessly, whether or not you're interested in what they have to say.

_____

_____

_____

4. The musician brought along a <u>dulcimer,</u> an instrument with metal strings.

_____

_____

_____

5. To give the tasteless stew some flavor, I added salt, pepper, mustard, and every other <u>condiment</u> I could find in the kitchen.

_____

_____

_____

6. The woman <u>vehemently</u> denied that she had done anything wrong. Over and over she shouted that she was innocent. The judge told her to calm down and lower her voice.

_____

_____

_____

7. After the rockslide, a huge boulder <u>obstructed</u> the entrance to the cave. There was no way out. We were trapped.

_____

_____

_____

8. The entire town turned out to greet the team, everyone cheering and laughing. "We're number one!" the crowd chanted wildly. Such <u>jubilation</u> was wonderful to be part of!

_____

_____

_____

9. We all wondered whether Mr. Vargas had been forced to attend the meeting or if he had come of his own <u>volition</u>.

_____

_____

_____

10. Brendan was a <u>petulant</u> young man, who became angry for the slightest reason. Disagreeing with him was a sure way to get into an argument.

_____

_____

_____

Think It Through

1. After the jury listened to the victim's <u>version</u> of what happened, they heard the doctor's account.

   Account is a synonym for **version**. Both words refer to a description of events presented from a particular viewpoint. First the jury heard the victim's description of events, then the doctor's.

2. The soldiers advanced cautiously, uncertain if the people of the village were <u>hostile</u> or friendly.

   The word **friendly** contrasts with the word **hostile**. (And the word **or** acts as a signal word.) **Hostile** means the opposite of **friendly,** or **unfriendly.** In the context of soldiers advancing toward a village, I can infer that the author means **"unfriendly"** in the sense of siding with the enemy.

3. Salesmen are the most <u>garrulous</u> creatures on earth. They talk endlessly, whether or not you're interested in what they have to say.

   The descriptive information in the second sentence helps me conclude that **garrulous** means "talkative". Checking the dictionary, I see I'm right. The dictionary also notes that **garrulous** is a disapproving term. It's usually used to describe someone who chatters on and on in a boring way.

4. The musician brought along a <u>dulcimer</u>, an instrument with metal strings.

   The sentence explains that a **dulcimer** is a stringed instrument. Since a "musician" brought it, I can reasonably assume that a dulcimer is a **musical** instrument, rather than, say, a scientific instrument.

5. To give the tasteless stew some flavor, I added salt, pepper, mustard, and every other <u>condiment</u> I could find in the kitchen.

> Salt, pepper, and mustard are examples that suggest a
> **condiment** must be a kind of spice. Checking the dictionary,
> I see I'm on the right track. A **condiment** is a spice, seasoning,
> or sauce used to add flavor to food.

6. The woman <u>vehemently</u> denied that she had done anything wrong. Over and over she shouted that she was innocent. The judge told her to calm down and lower her voice.

> Descriptive information in the second and third sentences helps
> me figure out that **vehemently** must mean "with intense feeling."
> For example, the woman is shouting, and the judge tells her to
> calm down.

7. After the rockslide, a huge boulder <u>obstructed</u> the entrance to the cave. There was no way out. We were trapped.

> The second and third sentences clearly suggest that
> **obstructed** means "blocked."

8. The entire town turned out to greet the team, everyone cheering and laughing. "We're number one!" the crowd chanted wildly. Such <u>jubilation</u> was wonderful to be part of!

> The first two sentences suggest that **jubilation** means great
> happiness, of the sort people feel at a victory celebration.
> Checking the dictionary, I see I'm correct: **jubilation** means "a
> feeling of joyful happiness or triumph."

9. We all wondered whether Mr. Vargas had been forced to attend the meeting or if he had come of his own <u>volition</u>.

The signal word **or** suggests an opposite or contrast. Here "come of his own **volition**" is in contrast to "had been forced." I can conclude that **volition** means "will." In other words, Mr. Vargas had either been forced to come or else he had come of his own free will.

10. Brendan was a <u>petulant</u> young man, who became angry for the slightest reason. Disagreeing with him was a sure way to get into an argument.

Petulant is explained by the second part of the first sentence. The second sentence reinforces the meaning. Someone who is **petulant** tends to get angry easily.

Activity J: Linking Skills

Answer the following question in a short paragraph. Support your answer with one or more examples.

In section 3-2 (pages 77-95), you learned about making inferences. In this section, you learned about using context to determine meaning. How are the two skills related?

_____

_____

_____

_____

_____

_____

REVIEW

Here is a brief summary of what you've learned in section 3-4. To review concepts or strategies in more detail, turn back to the pages indicated.

Concepts to Understand (pages114-115):

- *Context* refers to the words or sentences that come before and after a particular word. You can figure out the meaning of a word from its context.
- A word may have different meanings in different contexts. One meaning may be literal while another is figurative.
- Many words have more than one meaning. You can use context to figure out which meaning applies in a sentence.

Using context clues (pages 115-118):

- Use the surrounding sentences.
- Look for descriptive information.
- Look for an explanation.
- Look for examples.
- Look for a synonym.
- Look for an opposite or contrast.

TIP: If You Get Stuck, Use Your Best Judgment

If you're stumped by a multiple-choice question that asks for the meaning of a word, first eliminate the answer choices you think are wrong. Then focus on just the remaining choices. Try each one in the sentence context. The choice that seems to make the most sense is probably the correct answer.

PRACTICE

The selections and questions that follow will give you a chance to practice the reading strategies that you've learned in Part 3 and the test-taking strategies that you learned in Part 2. Because MCAS exam questions call for a combination of skills, practice questions touch on skills beyond those covered in just this section.

Reading Selection 1

The following selection is an excerpt from The Big Drink, *a book by journalist E. J. Kahn, Jr.. Read the excerpt and then answer the questions that follow.*

The Discovery of Coca-Cola
by E. J. Kahn, Jr.

1 The man who invented Coca-Cola was not a native Atlantan, but on the day of his funeral every drugstore in town testimonially shut up shop. He was John Styth Pemberton, born in 1833 in Knoxville, Georgia, eighty miles away. Sometimes known as Doctor, Pemberton was a pharmacist who, during the Civil War, led a cavalry troop under General Joe Wheeler. He settled in Atlanta in 1869, and soon began brewing such patent medicines as Triplex Liver Pills and Globe of Flower Cough Syrup. In 1885, he registered a trademark for something called French Wine Coca—Ideal Nerve and Tonic Stimulant; a few months later he formed the Pemberton Chemical Company, and recruited the service of a bookkeeper name Frank M. Robinson, who not only had a good head for figures but, attached to it, so exceptional a nose that he could audit the composition of a batch of syrup merely by sniffing it. In 1866—a year in which, as contemporary Coca-Cola officials like to point out, Conan Doyle unveiled Sherlock Holmes and France unveiled the Statue of Liberty—Pemberton unveiled a syrup that he called Coca-Cola. It was a modification of his French Wine Coca. He had taken out the wine and added a pinch of caffeine, and, when the end product tasted awful, had thrown in some extract of cola (or Kola) nut and a few other oils, blending the mixture in a three-legged iron pot in his backyard and swishing it around with an oar. He distributed it to soda fountains in used beer bottles, and Robinson, with his flowing bookkeeper's script, presently devised a label, on which "Coca-Cola" was written in the fashion that is still employed. Pemberton looked upon his concoction less as a refreshment than as a headache cure, especially for people whose throbbing temples could be traced to overindulgence. On a morning late in 1886, one such victim of the night before dragged himself into an Atlanta drugstore and asked for a dollop of Coca-Cola. Druggists customarily stirred a teaspoonful of syrup into a

glass of water, but in this instance the factotum on duty was too lazy to walk to the fresh-water tap, a couple of feet off. Instead, he mixed the syrup with some charged water, which was closer at hand. The suffering customer perked up almost at once, and word quickly spread that the best Coca-Cola was a fizzy one.

Multiple-Choice Questions

1. In line 2, what does the word *testimonially* mean?

   A. for legal reasons

   B. as a show of respect

   C. quickly

   D. to attract customers

2. In line 16, the word *modification* means

   A. changed form.

   B. exact copy.

   C. antidote.

   D. more expensive product.

3. In line 24, what does the word *concoction* mean?

   A. business

   B. fate

   C. mixture

   D. good fortune

4. In line 26, the word *dollop* means

   A. small amount.

   B. bottle.

   C. can.

   D. one dollar's worth.

5. Which word is closest to the meaning of *factotum* in line 28?

    A. policeman

    B. customer

    C. inventor

    D. worker

6. Which word is closest to the meaning of *charged* in line 30?

    A. expensive

    B. electric

    C. carbonated

    D. explosive

7. Which event did **not** occur in 1886?

    A. France unveiled the Statue of Liberty.

    B. Pemberton registered a trademark for "French Wine Coca."

    C. Coca-Cola syrup was introduced.

    D. The author Arthur Conan Doyle introduced Sherlock Holmes.

8. According to the author, the discovery of Coca-Cola

    A. was the result of scientific research.

    B. actually took place in France.

    C. was accidental.

    D. occurred on the day of John Styth Pemberton's funeral.

The following article is from a newspaper. Read the article and then answer the questions that follow.

To Create Another Earth, or Let It Be
by Seth Borenstein

1   Once humans get to Mars, then what?

    The red planet is a most inhospitable place for people to live. The air is 95 percent carbon dioxide, with nitrogen and argon the other major

2   elements. There's little atmospheric pressure; it's frigid, and ultra-windy. Experts say the planet could be shaped into something more Earthlike. But is it right to do that?

    The futuristic question of whether people should alter Mars' environment to make it more suitable is already stirring debate, steeped in centuries-old American history. The phrase "terraforming," fresh out of

3   science fiction, is used in the same discussions as the 19th-century phrase "manifest destiny."

    The fields of ethics, ecology, science and politics all mix in a mess

4   when it comes to the idea of making Mars habitable for humans.

    Changing a planet is already being done here on Earth, scientists and authors say. All humans have to do to Mars—and it isn't easy, but the

5   concept is simple to grasp—is start a runaway greenhouse effect there to warm it up and then introduce lots of plants to produce oxygen.

    People would set up factories to release massive amounts of fluorocarbons into the thin Martian atmosphere "with the conscious intent of polluting," said Mars Society founder Robert Zubrin. That could raise

6   the surface temperature from around 64 degrees below zero at night to about 45 degrees below zero at night. At the equator in daytime, temperatures already reach the 70s and 80s. That would allow for liquid water in the tropics, which is crucial to life.

    After 50 years, the atmosphere, now one-one hundredth the thickness of Earth's, would be up to one-third of Earth's. Over thousands of years, the

7   plants would take the carbon dioxide and gradually produce oxygen, said Zubrin, an engineer who has designed plans to go to Mars.

    "It's physically possible," Zubrin said. "It's not easy. It won't

8   be cheap."

    But is it right to do it if there's something else alive on Mars, even a

9   microbe deep underground?

    The late astronomer Carl Sagan, in his book "Cosmos," said

10   definitely not.

    "If there is life on Mars, I believe we should do nothing with Mars," Sagan said. "Mars then belongs to the Martians, even if the Martians are

11   only microbes."

12 But Zubrin and others say those microbes—while historic and worthy of study—shouldn't stand in the way of human progress. That's human nature, he said.

13 "It would be unnatural for us not to terraform Mars. It would be unlifelike," Zubrin said.

Multiple-Choice Questions

1. The author of this article begins by making what assumption?

   A. Martians are friendly.

   B. Human beings will travel to Mars.

   C. The climate of Mars is similar to Earth's.

   D. There is life on Mars.

2. Which definition is closest to the meaning of *inhospitable* in paragraph 2?

   A. located a great distance away

   B. not kind to strangers

   C. not providing comfortable conditions

   D. beyond the limits of space travel

3. In paragraph 3, what does the word *futuristic* mean?

   A. relating to the future

   B. controversial

   C. difficult to answer

   D. vague

4. *Terraforming* refers to

   A. building factories on other planets.

   B. using modern agricultural methods.

   C. reducing pollution in space.

   D. changing a planet's environment.

5. In paragraph 4, what does the word *habitable* mean?

    A. livable

    B. profitable

    C. customary

    D. enjoyable

6. What is the **main** purpose of this article?

    A. to persuade people to travel to Mars

    B. to explain the greenhouse effect

    C. to inform readers about life on Mars

    D. to describe a debate about Mars

Open-Response Question

7. The author describes the views of Robert Zubrin and Carl Sagan. How do their opinions differ? Use specific details from the article to support your answer.

_____

_____

_____

_____

_____

_____

3-5 Understanding an Author's Purpose and Point of View

CONCEPTS TO UNDERSTAND

All authors have a purpose for writing. For example, the author of a newspaper editorial tries to influence the opinion of readers. A television scriptwriter wants to entertain viewers.

In writing to achieve their purpose, authors usually reveal their point of view. Knowing how purpose and point of view are related yet different will help you understand both informational and literary selections.

- An author's purpose is his or her reason or goal for writing. Authors write for many purposes. Look at the illustration below.

WHY AUTHORS WRITE

to tell about real or imagined events

to inform readers

to entertain or amuse readers

to teach a lesson about life

to persuade readers to think or act in a certain way

to describe people, places, or things

- Although they may have a single main purpose, authors often accomplish more than one purpose. Suppose, for example, an author writes about his or her world travels. In addition to the main purpose of describing people and places, the author may inform readers about historical events. The author may include a persuasive message about the need for nations to work together.

- To achieve their writing purpose, authors include some ideas, facts, and details and omit others. They decide how to organize their content. They choose specific words to describe people, places, and events. By means of such decisions and choices, authors shape their written work.
- Through their writing, authors usually show their *point of view.* That is, they state or imply how they feel about their subject or theme.

AUTHOR'S PURPOSE	why the author writes
AUTHOR'S POINT OF VIEW	how the author feels about the subject or theme

- Purpose and point of view are always related, but exactly *how* they are related varies with the particular selection. Study the examples in the chart below.

How are Purpose and Point of View Related?

SELECTION	AUTHOR'S PURPOSE	Author's Point of View
Informational:		
essay	to persuade readers to do volunteer work in their community	feels that people have a moral responsibility to help one another
article	to explain the benefits and dangers of the Internet	thinks that computer users don't know as much about the Internet as they should
Literary:		
short story	to show that many things in life are more important than money	believes that people are too concerned with getting rich
poem	to describe the excitement of city life	believes that living in the city is preferable to living in the country

Answer in your own words: What is the difference between an author's purpose and point of view?

_____

_____

_____

Activity K: Examining Purpose and Point of View

1. Read an editorial in a newspaper or magazine. Summarize the author's key points below.

   Name of editorial/column: _____

   Name and date of newspaper/magazine:

   _____

   Author's key points:

   _____

   _____

   _____

2. Why do you think the author wrote the editorial? Be specific.

   _____

   _____

   _____

3. How does the author feel about his or her subject? What makes you think so?

   _____

   _____

   _____

Telling Fact From Opinion

- Authors use facts to support their views, but they often mix facts with opinions. It's important to be able to tell them apart.
- A *fact* is something known to be true. Facts are based on information that can be verified (shown to be true). A *statement of fact* can be proved.
- An *opinion* is a belief, judgment, or conclusion based on what someone thinks. A *statement of opinion* can't be proved or disproved.

Facts: Boston is the capital of Massachusetts and the largest city in New England.

Opinions: Boston is the most fascinating and exciting city in all of New England.

- Opinions alone cannot prove a point, because you can agree or disagree with an opinion. Authors must use facts to support their opinions and prove their arguments.
- When you read a statement of opinion, look for facts that support it. Often the statement of opinion is the topic sentence of a paragraph and is followed by supporting facts.

Opinion (topic sentence):
People should not drive when they are taking medication.

Supporting facts:
Some doctor-prescribed medications contain narcotic drugs. Even "harmless" over-the-counter drugs can cause drowsiness and impair a person's driving ability and judgment.

READING STRATEGIES: UNDERSTANDING PURPOSE AND POINT OF VIEW

Use the following strategies to help you understand an author's purpose and point of view.

- **Identify key ideas.** To understand an author's purpose and point of view, you have to identify or infer the central point and main ideas of a selection. (To review how, see section 3-1, *Identifying Key Ideas and Information,* and section 3-2, *Making Inferences and Drawing Conclusions.*)

- **Consider why the author wrote the selection.** Did he or she want to influence your opinion? Present information? Make you laugh? Describe a particular event?
- **Think about the structure of the selection.** How an author organizes ideas and information reveals what he or she considers most important. What facts or details does the author seem to stress most?
- **Notice the elements of fiction, nonfiction, and poetry.** For example, authors can reveal their feelings through the use of figurative language, irony, and exaggeration. You'll read about the elements of fiction, nonfiction, and poetery in section 3–6.
- **Pay attention to word choice.** As discussed in section 3-2 (page 82), language can show people and events in either a positive or a negative light. For example, *crowd* and mob both refer to a large group of people, but mob has a negative connotation (implied meaning).
- **Notice what the author includes and omits.** For example, an author may describe in great detail the pleasures of mountain climbing but say nothing of the dangers. What would that suggest about the author's purpose and point of view?

Activity L: Using the Strategies

Reread the editorial that you used for *Activity K* (page 133). How can the above strategies help you understand the author's purpose and point of view? Include specific details or examples from the editorial to support your answer.

_____

_____

_____

APPLY YOUR KNOWLEDGE

- The following selection is an excerpt from a newspaper column. Read the passage and answer the questions. Use the reading strategies that you've learned.
- After you have finished, read the *Think It Through* that follows to see how one student answered the questions.

Good Morning, Kids

It's Saturday morning. Across the nation, young children are sprawled in front of television sets. They're ready to view their favorite programs, the ones they see every Saturday and often watch during

1   the week as well.

Images bombard these young viewers, fast-moving pictures filled with bright colors and accompanied by loud sounds. Crazed animated villains blow up buildings with ray guns or obliterate them with bombs. Evil super-robots demolish entire cities, as people run screaming through the

2   streets.Cartoon characters pound one another with baseball bats, shoot each other with shotguns, and fling each other off cliffs. Good guys do battle with bad guys, sometimes using fists and feet, other times using the latest in high-tech weaponry. The mayhem and murder are interrupted only by commercials selling action figures and fast food.

Research studies have shown that some of the most popular children's programs are five times more violent than shows televised during prime

3   time. Some years ago, one study even identified "Bugs Bunny— Roadrunner" as the single most violent program on television.

And adults wonder why children seem "desensitized" to violence and suffering in the real world, why kids sometimes respond with violence

4   themselves. Spend an hour or two watching children's television, and the answer comes through as clearly as a gunshot.

1. What is the central point of this selection?

_____

_____

_____

2. What is the author's purpose?

_____

_____

_____

3. How does the author feel about the subject of children's television? How can you tell?

_____

_____

_____

4. How does the author's choice of language help to express the author's point of view?

_____

_____

_____

5. What literary technique does the author use in the last sentence? Why do you think the author uses it?

_____

_____

_____

Think It Through

1. What is the central point of this selection?

   The central point is that children's TV shows so much violence that it's no wonder kids become "desensitized" to real violence and may even act violently themselves.

2. What is the author's purpose?

   The author's purpose is to make people aware of what children's TV is really like.

3. How does the author feel about the subject of children's television? How can you tell?

The author is highly critical of children's TV. The author's negative feeling's are shown through facts, details, and examples in paragraphs 2 and 3, which relate directly to the ideas suggested in paragraph 4.

4. How does the author's choice of language help to express the author's point of view?

The author uses vivid language that has a negative association: bombard, obliterate, screaming through the streets, mayhem and murder. Such language emphasizes the violent nature of the examples.

5. What literary technique does the author use in the last sentence? Why do you think the author uses it?

In the last sentence, the author writes that "the answer comes through as clearly as a gunshot." This comparison to a gunshot is a simile. The author uses it to dramatically make the point about violence in children's television.

APPLY YOUR KNOWLEDGE

- The following selection is an excerpt from an article called "Moving into Forest Park." Read the passage and answer the questions. Use the reading strategies that you've learned.
- After you have finished, read the *Think It Through* that follows to see how one student answered the questions.

Moving into Forest Park

1   In Nigeria, the Momassa family had heard from those who journeyed to America of a place called Forest Park. The promised land was not without its hardship, people said, but in Forest Park the fellowship of Africans made life's challenges easier to face.

2   Since arriving several months ago and moving into one of the six buildings of the Forest Park development, Mohammed Momassa and his sons have prayed every day in a two-bedroom, ground-floor apartment that was converted into a mosque. They pray beside immigrants from Senegal, Mali, Egypt, and the Ivory Coast.

3   In another apartment in a nearby building, Miriam Blumenthal and two other Jewish refugees from the former Soviet Union discuss the synagogue expected to open in Forest Park next month.

4   Since general manager Carlos Gallarga came to Forest Park four years ago, he has worked to knit the development's diverse population into a community. For teenagers, he added a soccer field and a basketball court. For retired residents, he set aside an area for a vegetable garden. For families, he organizes barbecues.

5   On a recent afternoon, Mrs. Blumenthal watched as her son played soccer with Tariq Momassa and a group of other children from Cuba, Korea, and Croatia. When the Blumenthals first came to Forest Park, theirs was the only Jewish family on a floor occupied by immigrant families from Africa, Asia, and the Caribbean. "They helped us . . . gave us clothes and furniture," Mrs. Blumenthal said. "Now our children play together. I like that."

1. What was the author's purpose in writing this selection? Give reasons for your answer.

    _____

    _____

    _____

2. Why do you think the author included the quoted words of Mrs. Blumenthal in paragraph 5?

    _____

    _____

    _____

3. How does the author's choice of supporting information send an implied message to the reader?

_____

_____

_____

Think It Through

1. What was the author's purpose in writing this selection? Give reasons for your answer.

The author probably wants to show how it's possible to join a "diverse population into a community." All the examples and details the author provides support the idea that people from different backgrounds can get along.

2. Why do you think the author included the quoted words of Mrs. Blumenthal in paragraph 5?

Mrs. Blumenthal's words help to emphasize the idea that the people of Forest Park, as different as they are, live in harmony and help one another. Using a quotation also adds a human touch to the article.

3. How does the author's choice of supporting information send an implied message to the reader?

The examples and other supporting information suggest that the author feels very positively about Forest Park. The implied message is that people can overcome or set aside their cultural differences.

TIP: Look to the Characters in Literary Works

Identifying an author's purpose and point of view may require extra effort with literary works, such as short stories and novels. Think carefully about the main characters. For example, what happens to the protagonist (central character)? Why does this happen? What might this outcome suggest about the author's purpose and point of view?

REVIEW

Here is a brief summary of what you've learned in section 3-5. To review concepts or strategies in more detail, turn back to the pages indicated.

Concepts to Understand (pages 131-133):

- An author's *purpose* is his or her reason or goal for writing.
- To achieve their purpose, authors decide what information to include or omit, how to organize their content, and what descriptive language to use. These decisions shape the written work.
- Through their writing, authors usually state or imply their *point of view*—how they feel about their subject or theme.

Understanding an author's purpose and point of view (pages 134-135):

- Identify key ideas.
- Consider why the author wrote the selection.
- Think about the structure of the selection.
- Notice the elements of fiction, nonfiction, and poetry.
- Pay attention to word choice.
- Notice what the author includes and omits.

PRACTICE

The selections and questions that follow will give you a chance to practice the reading strategies that you've learned in Part 3 and the test-taking strategies that you learned in Part 2. Because MCAS exam questions call for a combination of skills, practice questions touch on skills beyond those covered in just this section.

Reading Selection 1

In the following essay, the author explains why she finds her life satisfying. Read the essay carefully. Then answer the questions that follow.

The Rewards of Living a Solitary Life
by May Sarton

The other day an acquaintance of mine, a gregarious and charming man, told me he had found himself unexpectedly alone in New York for an hour or two between appointments. He went to the Whitney [Museum] and spent the "empty" time looking at things in solitary bliss.

1   For him it proved to be a shock nearly as great as falling in love to discover that he could enjoy himself so much alone.

What had he been afraid of, I asked myself? That, suddenly alone, he would discover that he bored himself, or that there was, quite simply, no self there to meet? But having taken the plunge, he is now on the brink of adventure; he is about to be launched into his own inner space, space as immense, unexplored, and sometimes frightening as outer space to the

2   astronaut. His every perception will come to him with a new freshness and, for a time, seem startlingly original. For anyone who can see things for himself with a naked eye becomes, for a moment or two, something of a genius. With another human being present vision becomes double vision, inevitably. We are busy wondering, what does my companion see or think of this, and what do I think of it? the original impact gets lost, or diffused.

"Music I heard with you was more than music."* Exactly. And

3   therefore music itself can only be heard alone. Solitude is the salt of personhood. It brings out the authentic flavor of every experience.

"Alone one is never lonely: the spirit adventures, walking/In a quiet

4   garden, in a cool house, abiding single there."

Loneliness is most acutely felt with other people, for with others, even with a lover sometimes, we suffer from our differences of taste,

5   temperament, mood. Human intercourse often demands that we soften the edge of perception, or withdraw at the very instant of personal truth for fear of hurting, or of being inappropriately present, which is to say naked,

A line from Conrad Aiken's poem, "Bread and Music"

in a social situation. Alone we can afford to be wholly whatever we are, and to feel whatever we feel absolutely. That is a great luxury!

For me the most interesting thing about a solitary life, and mine has been that for the last twenty years, is that it becomes increasingly rewarding. When I can wake up and watch the sun rise over the ocean,

6 as I do most days, and know that I have an entire day ahead, uninterrupted, in which to write a few pages, take a walk with my dog, lie down in the afternoon for a long think (why does one think better in a horizontal position?), read and listen to music, I am flooded with happiness.

I am lonely only when I am overtired, when I have worked too long without a break, when for the time being I feel empty and need filling up.

7 And I am lonely sometimes when I come back home after a lecture trip, when I have seen a lot of people and talked a lot, and am full to the brim with experience that needs to be sorted out.

Then for a little while the house feels huge and empty, and I wonder where my self is hiding. It has to be recaptured slowly by watering the

8 plants, perhaps, and looking again at each one as though it were a person, by feeding the two cats, by cooking a meal.

It takes a while, as I watch the surf blowing up in fountains at the end of the field, but the moment comes when the world falls away, and the self

9 emerges again from the deep unconscious, bringing back all I have recently experienced to be explored and slowly understood, when I can converse again with my hidden powers, and so grow, and so be renewed, till death do us part.

Multiple-Choice Questions

1. Which definition comes closest to the meaning of the phrase "in solitary bliss" in paragraph 1?

    A. happily alone

    B. feeling bored

    C. isolated and unhappy

    D. in confusion

2. In paragraph 1, why does the man's visit to the Whitney Museum turn out "to be a shock"?

    A. He had expected to dislike the museum.

    B. He fell in love.

    C. He was surprised to have so much fun by himself.

    D. He was not expecting to be so bored.

3. In paragraph 3, the author writes, "Solitude is the salt of personhood. It brings out the authentic flavor of every experience." The author is making her point by using

   A. alliteration.

   B. personification.

   C. metaphor.

   D. hyperbole.

4. According to the author, a key benefit of living alone is that people

   A. can own pets.

   B. don't have to talk to anyone.

   C. can sleep late.

   D. are free to be themselves.

5. The purpose of this essay is to

   A. persuade people to leave their spouses.

   B. describe positive aspects of living alone.

   C. amuse readers.

   D. inform readers about their rights.

6. The author expresses her feeling that the solitary life

   A. is appropriate for everyone.

   B. makes her happy.

   C. becomes less rewarding as one gets older.

   D. is a lonely life.

Open-Response Question

7. Using information from the essay, explain what the author believes are "the rewards of living a solitary life."

_____

_____

_____

_____

_____

_____

Read the poem "Progress." Think about how the poet feels about the scene he is describing. Then answer the questions that follow.

Progress

by John Sterling Harris

The old church is down,
And where it stood
Lie scattered chunks of plaster
On dry rough-graded ground
Shielded from the rain a hundred years;   5
The dump trucks hauled away the scraps
Of age-darkened wood with
Many layers of white and ivory paint;
The bricks of the new addition,
Only half a century old,   10
Were carefully scraped of mortar
And stacked in cubical piles—
There is a good demand for antique brick
To build the prosperous houses on the hill;
The huge old ceiling beams   15
And the rough-sawn red pine rafters,
Too big to use, too hard to cut,
Will make fence rails
And cattle shelters somewhere;
But the handmade adobe bricks   20
Of the chapel's yard-thick walls
Have no modern use;
The dozer knocks them down,
Not easily, but still too quickly
To return to the earth they came from.   25

It was always there,
And the schools and stores came later,
Because it was there;
Now the street is naked for its loss.

The officials point with pride   30
To the bright glass replacement up the street,
Praise the classrooms,
The long carpeted hallways
And the tall aluminum steeple
That has no bell;   35
They walk with relief over the old site
With its fearsome past all hauled away
And talk with the service station man
About his plans.

Multiple-Choice Questions

1. What is the **main** subject of this poem?

   A. the replacement of an old church

   B. the development of improved building materials

   C. the demand for antique brick

   D. the use of modern construction techniques

2. What is the poet's attitude toward what he is describing?

   A. He disapproves.

   B. He is delighted.

   C. He thinks the change is long overdue.

   D. He is amused.

3. Which part of the church will **not** be reused?

   A. the antique bricks of the addition

   B. the ceiling beams

   C. the pine rafters

   D. the handmade adobe bricks

4. The title of this poem is an example of

   A. personification.

   B. hyperbole.

   C. irony.

   D. onomatopoeia.j149

Open-Response Question

5. Compare the new church with the old one. Use specific details from the poem to make your comparison.

_____

_____

_____

_____

_____

_____

3-6 Analyzing Elements of Fiction, Nonfiction, and Poetry

CONCEPTS TO UNDERSTAND

The MCAS exam contains both fiction and nonfiction reading selections. These selections come from a variety of sources.

SOURCES OF READING SELECTIONS		
Literary Works	**Informational Works**	
short stories	nonfiction books	speeches
novels	essays	editorials
poetry	letters	diary entries
plays	biographies	autobiographies
myths	interviews	newspaper articles
fables		

- Every literary and informational work is a combination of elements. What makes each work unique is the way the author blends these elements to communicate ideas and feelings.
- Some elements are generally associated with works of fiction. Others are usually found in works of nonfiction. However, there are no absolute rules. For example, a science article may use vivid imagery to describe events, while a novel may present scientific information.

For the MCAS exam, you should be able to identify and analyze a wide range of elements of fiction, nonfiction, and poetry. Study pages150-152.

Recognizing Elements of Fiction, Nonfiction, and Poetry

- **Allegory** is the representation of ideas or moral principles by means of symbolic characters, events, or objects. For example, the fables of Aesop use allegory to teach lessons about life.

- **Alliteration** is the repetition of an initial (usually consonant) sound, as in *swift, silent serpent.*

- **Characterization** is the creation and development of **characters,** the people who carry on the action in a literary work.

- **Figurative language** is words used in an imaginative, non-literal sense. Similes and metaphors (see below) are examples of figurative language.

- **Figures of speech** are forms of expression in which the author uses language in an imaginative, non-literal sense to make a comparison or produce a desired effect.

  A **simile** is a comparison using *like* or *as.*

  Examples: *Her eyes gleamed like stars. The house was as large as a castle.*

  A **metaphor** is an implied comparison that does not use *like* or *as.*

  Example: *They were tigers on the playing field, ferociously mauling their opponents.*

  Personification is the giving of human qualities to objects, ideas, or animals.

  Example: *The sun smiled down on the village.*

  Hyperbole, or **exaggeration,** is overstatement for the purpose of emphasis.

  Example: *His ears were so sharp he could hear dogs bark in the next county.*

  Onomatopoeia is words that sound like the things they name.

  Examples: *bang, buzz, crackle, sizzle, hiss, murmur, roar.*

Recognizing Elements of Fiction, Nonfiction, and Poetry

An **oxymoron** is a combination of two contradictory words.

Examples: *deafening silence, a definite possibility.*

- **Flashback** refers to a scene that shows an earlier event, often one that happened before the opening scene of a literary work. For example, a novelist may include a flashback to show an event that happened during the childhood of an adult character.

- **Foreshadowing** is the suggestion of events to come. For example, gray clouds at the beginning of a story may foreshadow a storm that occurs later.

- **Imagery** is description or figurative language. Authors create vivid **images,** or word pictures, through their creative use of language. These images may appeal to the five senses.

  Examples: *Thick tree roots clutched the ground like gnarled fingers. The frightened screech of an unseen animal tore through the night.*

- **Irony** is a situation or event that is the opposite of what is or might be expected. For example, it would be *ironic* if a lifeguard had to be saved from drowning.

  Irony can also be an attitude or intention that is the opposite of what is actually meant, as when a latecomer is sarcastically told, "We're so glad you could join us!"

- **Mood** is the atmosphere or feeling of a work. For example, the mood may be joyful, gloomy, or suspenseful.

- The **plot** of a short story, novel, or other literary work is the sequence of events that take place.

- **Point of view** may be how a story is told. For example, in *first-person* point of view, the narrator himself or herself tells the story and may participate in events. Works written in the first person use pronouns such as *I, me,* and *my.* In third-person point of view, the author is an outside observer who does not take part in events. Authors using third-person point of view can describe the thoughts and actions of all characters.

Recognizing Elements of Fiction, Nonfiction, and Poetry

Point of view can also refer to how an author feels about his or her subject or theme. To review this meaning of the term, see section 3-5, *Understanding an Author's Purpose and Point of View.*

- **Repetition** is the repeating of a word or group of words for effect. For example, Archibald MacLeish's poem "The End of the World" concludes with these lines:

  There in the sudden blackness the black pall
  Of nothing, nothing, nothing—nothing at all.

- A **rhetorical question** is asked only for effect or to make a statement, not to get an answer.

  Example: *How much longer will we put up with this injustice? Isn't it time that we took action?*

- **Satire** is writing that uses humor, irony, or wit to attack or make fun of something, such as people's follies or vices.

- **Setting** is the time and place in which events occur. For example, the setting of Shakespeare's play *Macbeth* is eleventh-century Scotland.

- **Structure** refers to how the parts of a work are organized and arranged. For example, the structure of a novel or biography may be based on chronological (time) order with occasional flashbacks (see page 151). The structure of poetry includes the number, form, and pattern of lines and stanzas.

- **Symbolism** is the representation of ideas or things by symbols. A **symbol** is something that stands for something else. For example, an author may use a rose as a symbol of beauty or a snake as a symbol of evil.

- The **theme** (or **central point**) is the principal point of a work, the main focus or underlying meaning. For example, many authors have written on the theme that life is short, so everyone must make the most of each day. To review this term in detail, see section 3-1, *Identifying Key Ideas and Information.*

- **Tone** is the attitude or viewpoint that an author shows toward his or her subject. For example, tone may be serious, sympathetic, optimistic, or angry.

Activity M: Linking Literary Elements

Reread "The Problem with Teenagers" on page 86. Then answer the questions below.

1. Explain the irony in this selection.

_____

_____

_____

2. How does the author's use of irony help to communicate the central point?

_____

_____

_____

READING STRATEGIES:
ANALYZING ELEMENTS OF FICTION, NONFICTION, AND POETRY

The following strategies will help you interpret reading selections and understand the author's meaning.

- **Make inferences.** Reading selections, especially fictional works and poetry, blend stated and implied ideas. To understand an author's meaning, look for both. For example, when reading poetry, look for symbolism behind the poet's words and images.

  You can also apply your inference skills to other elements, such as setting and mood. For example, an opening paragraph that describes a creepy old house on a stormy night may suggest a dark mood for a short story.

  To review strategies for making inferences, refer to section 3-2, *Making Inferences and Drawing Conclusions* (pages 80-82). For tips on reading poetry, review the box on page 17.

- **Think about characterization and plot.** Authors of literary works reveal their ideas, feelings, and values through characters and plot. The events and conversations in a story don't just "happen." The author *makes* them happen, and he or she does so for a reason. Try to figure out what that reason is.

As you read, ask yourself thought-provoking questions about characters and plot. Here are some examples:

What is the purpose/importance of this scene?

What is the author showing with this plot development?

How does the author feel about this character?

Why does this character act this way?

Why does the author include this dialogue?

Why does the author end the story this way?

- **Pay attention to language.** Authors of both informative and literary works use imagery, figurative language, repetition, and other elements to express thoughts and feelings. Read carefully to grasp the full meaning that an author wants to convey.

- **Examine structure.** Are events described in the order they happened, or are the most recent events described first? Are causes presented before effects? Do facts and details build up to a conclusion? The answers to such questions will give you insight into the author's purpose and central point. (To read about methods of organization, refer to pages 229-230.)

- **Consider how elements work together.** Authors achieve various effects by combining elements. For instance, an author may use exaggeration and irony to write a satire about modern society. In order to fully appreciate a literary or informational work, be aware of how all the pieces come together to form the whole.

Activity N: Exploring Plot and Character

Here is the beginning of a plot for a short story:

A young woman and a young man meet and fall in love. They want to get married, but the woman's parents feel that the man is not good enough for their daughter. They refuse to approve the marriage.

Here are three different ways an author might develop the plot:

Possibility #1: The woman tries to persuade her parents but fails. She decides that she has no choice but to end the relationship, rather than go against her parents' wishes.

Possibility #2: The woman warns her parents that if they do not give their approval, she and her boyfriend will get married anyway.

Possibility #3: The woman is unable to win her parents' approval, but she feels that she cannot give up the man she loves. She doesn't know what to do. Then her boyfriend insists that she must "choose them or me."

1. For each of the three possible plots, briefly describe what events might follow and how the story might end.

   Possibility #1:

   _____

   _____

   _____

   Possibility #2:

   _____

   _____

   _____

   Possibility #3:

   _____

   _____

   _____

2. What idea(s) could you convey to readers through the plot events you described?

Possibility #1:

_____

_____

_____

Possibility #2:

_____

_____

_____

Possibility #3:

_____

_____

_____

_____

3. Although your three plots all start the same way, differences in their development affect both characters and theme. Explain why this is true.

_____

_____

_____

APPLY YOUR KNOWLEDGE

- Read the following poem, and answer the questions. Use the reading strategies that you've learned. For tips on reading poetry, review the box on page 17.
- After you have finished, read the *Think It Through* that follows to see how one student answered the questions.

Apartment House
by Gerald Raftery

A filing-cabinet of human lives
Where people swarm like bees in tunneled hives,
Each to his own cell in the towered comb,
Identical and cramped—we call it home.

1. To what two things does the poet compare an apartment house?

_____

_____

_____

2. How does the simile in line 2 contribute to the meaning of the poem?

_____

_____

_____

3. How does the poet use imagery to convey his ideas?

_____

_____

_____

4. How would you describe the tone of the poem?

_____

_____

_____

Think It Through

1. To what two things does the poet compare an apartment house?

> In line 1, the poet compares the apartment house to a filing
> cabinet. In line 3, the poet compares it to a "towered comb"—
> that is, a honeycomb. (Both comparisons are metaphors. A
> metaphor is an implied comparison made without using the
> words like or as.)

2. How does the simile in line 2 contribute to the meaning of
the poem?

> In line 2, the poet says that "people swarm like bees in tunneled
> hives." This simile suggests an image of many people crowding
> around in a small area. This image relates directly to the poem's
> theme.

3. How does the poet use imagery to convey his ideas?

> The poet uses two main images: the filing cabinet and the
> honeycomb. Both images suggest many individuals crowded
> together inside one structure—the apartment house.

> In line 3, the poet uses the word cell. This word may have a
> double meaning. First, it refers to a cell, or compartment, in a
> honeycomb. Second, it suggests a jail cell. Both meanings help
> to convey the idea of people being enclosed in small spaces.

4. How would you describe the tone of the poem?

> Tone is an author's attitude toward his or her subject. In this
> poem, I think that the poet's attitude toward apartment houses
> is mixed.
>
> On the one hand, the imagery doesn't paint a very positive
> picture of life in an apartment house. Neither does the last line,
> where the poet describes the cells as "identical and cramped."
> However, the last four words—"we call it home"—do seem to
> have a positive feeling. It's as if the poet is saying, "an
> apartment house may have drawbacks, but it's still home."

TIP: Narrative Works Tell a Story

A narrative is a work that tells a story. Narrative, narration, and
narrator all come from a Latin word meaning "tell."

A narrative work may be literary or informational, fiction or
nonfiction. For example, short stories, fables, biographies, and
eyewitness accounts of history are all narrative works.

APPLY YOUR KNOWLEDGE

- The following selection is an excerpt from an essay that
  appeared in a magazine. Read the passage and answer the
  questions. Use the reading strategies that you've learned.
- After you have finished, read the *Think It Through* that follows
  to see how one student answered the questions.

Rambos of the Road

by Martin Gottfried

1   A most amazing example of driver rage occurred recently at the Manhattan end of the Lincoln Tunnel. We were four cars abreast, stopped at a traffic light. And there was no moving even when the light had changed. A bus had stopped in the cross traffic, blocking our paths: it was a normal-for-New-York-City gridlock. Perhaps impatient, perhaps late for important appointments, three of us nonetheless accepted what, after all, we could not alter. One, however, would not. He would not be helpless. He would go where he was going even if he couldn't get there. A Wall Street type in suit and tie, he got out of his car and strode toward the bus, rapping smartly on its door.

2   When they opened, he exchanged words with the driver. The doors folded shut. He then stepped in front of the bus, took hold of one of its large windshield wipers and broke it.

3   The bus doors reopened and the driver appeared, apparently giving the fellow a good piece of his mind. If so, the lecture was wasted, for the man started his car and proceeded to drive directly *into the bus*. He rammed it. Even though the point at which he struck the bus, the folding doors, was its most vulnerable point, ramming the side of a bus with your car has to rank very high on a futility index. My first thought was that it had to be a rented car.

4   To tell the truth, I could not believe my eyes. The bus driver opened his doors as much as they could be opened and he stepped directly onto the hood of the attacking car, jumping up and down with both his feet. He then retreated into the bus, closing the doors behind him. Obviously a man of action, the car driver backed up and rammed the bus again. How this exercise in absurdity would have been resolved none of us will ever know for at that point the traffic unclogged and the bus moved on. And the rest of us, we passives of the world, proceeded, our cars crossing a field of battle as if nothing untoward had happened.

5   It is tempting to blame such belligerent, uncivil and even neurotic behavior on the nuts of the world, but in our cars we all become a little crazy. How many of us speed up when a driver signals his intention of pulling in front of us? Are we resentful and anxious to pass him? How many of us try to squeeze in, or race along the shoulder at a lane merger? We may not jump on hoods but driving the gantlet, we seethe, cursing not so silently in the safety of our steel bodies on wheels—fortresses for cowards.

1. In paragraph 1, how is the description of the angry driver more literary than informational in nature?

_____

_____

_____

2. The author wrote this essay from the first-person point of view. Was this a wise choice? Why or why not?

_____

_____

_____

_____

3. In paragraph 4, what idea does the author support with three rhetorical questions?

_____

_____

_____

4. What does the author mean at the end of paragraph 4 when he uses the figure of speech "fortresses for cowards"?

_____

_____

_____

 ## Think It Through

1. In paragraph 1, how is the description of the angry driver more "literary" than "informational" in nature?

Instead of just referring to him as an angry man, the narrator describes him the way a fiction author might describe a character: "He would not be helpless. He would go where he was going even if he couldn't get there. A Wall Street type in suit and tie."

2. The author wrote this essay from the first-person point of view. Was this a wise choice? Why or why not?

I think that the first-person point of view was a wise choice because it makes the essay more personal and helps readers get involved. For example, when the narrator writes in paragraph 3 that "I could not believe my eyes," I really understood the feeling.

3. In paragraph 4, what idea does the author support with three rhetorical questions?

The author uses the rhetorical questions to support the idea that "in our cars we all become a little crazy."

4. What does the author mean at the end of paragraph 4 when he uses the figure of speech "fortresses for cowards"?

"Fortresses for cowards" is a metaphor. The author is comparing being safely inside a car with being safely inside a fortress. The author uses the word cowards to refer to people who behave badly while driving only because they are safely inside their cars.

Activity O: Exploring Elements of Fiction, Nonfiction, and Poetry

Work with a small group of students. Each group member in turn should share a brief favorite literary or informational selection (or excerpt). Then, as a group, discuss and analyze how the author of each selection used elements of fiction, nonfiction, and poetry to convey ideas.

Identify each selection, and then discuss the following questions:

Title: _____

Author: _____

Genre: _____

- What is the theme or central point of the selection?
- How does the author use elements of fiction, nonfiction, and poetry to convey the theme or central point?
- What specific elements of fiction, nonfiction, and poetry does the author use?

REVIEW

Here is a brief summary of what you've learned in section 3-6. To review concepts or strategies in more detail, turn back to the pages indicated.

Concepts to Understand (pages 149-152):

- Every literary and informational work is a unique combination of elements.
- Some elements are generally associated with works of fiction, while others usually appear in works of nonfiction. However, there are no absolute rules.
- To review elements of fiction, nonfiction, and poetry see pages 150-152.

Analyzing elements of fiction, nonfiction, and poetry (pages 153-154):

- Make inferences.
- Think about characterization and plot.
- Pay attention to language.
- Examine structure.
- Consider how elements work together.

PRACTICE

The selections and questions that follow will give you a chance to practice the reading strategies that you've learned in Part 3 and the test-taking strategies that you learned in Part 2. Because MCAS exam questions call for a combination of skills, practice questions touch on skills beyond those covered in just this section.

Reading Selection 1

In this excerpt, Richard Rodriguez, a Mexican American, describes the summer job that he took to help him understand the lives of Mexican laborers he had seen working. As you read, notice how the author uses details to make his description come alive. When you have finished reading, answer the questions that follow.

Hunger of Memory
by Richard Rodriguez

1 It was at Stanford, one day near the end of my senior year, that a friend told me about a summer construction job he knew was available. I was quickly alert. Desire uncoiled within me. My friend said that he knew I had been looking for summer employment. He knew I needed some money. Almost apologetically he explained: It was something I probably wouldn't be interested in, but a friend of his, a contractor, needed someone for the summer to do menial jobs. There would be lots of shoveling and raking and sweeping. Nothing too hard. But nothing more interesting either. Still, the pay would be good. Did I want it? Or did I know someone who did?

2 I did. Yes, I said, surprised to hear myself say it.

3 In the weeks following, friends cautioned that I had no idea how hard physical labor really is. ("You only *think* you know what it is like to shovel for eight hours straight.") Their objections seemed to me challenges. They resolved the issue. I became happy with my plan. I decided, however, not to tell my parents. I wouldn't tell my mother because I could guess her worried reaction. I would tell my father only after the summer was over, when I could announce that, after all, I did know what "real work" is like.

4 The day I met the contractor (a Princeton graduate, it turned out), he asked me whether I had done any physical labor before. "In high school, during the summer," I lied. And although he seemed to regard me with skepticism, he decided to give me a try. Several days later, expectant, I arrived at my first construction site. I would take off my shirt to the sun. And at last grasp desired sensation. No longer afraid. At last become like a *bracero.** "We need those tree stumps out of here by tomorrow," the contractor said. I started to work.

I labored with excitement that first morning—and all the days after. The work was harder than I could have expected. But it was never as tedious as my friend had warned me it would be. There was too much physical pleasure in the labor. Especially early in the day, I would be most alert to the sensations of movement and straining. Beginning around seven each morning (when the air was still damp but the scent of weeds and dry earth anticipated the heat of the sun), I would feel my body resist the first thrusts of the shovel. My arms, tightened by sleep, would gradually loosen; after only several minutes, sweat would gather in beads on my forehead and then—a short while later—I would feel my chest silky with sweat in the

5   breeze. I would return to my work. A nervous spark of pain would fly up my arm and settle to burn like an ember in the thick of my shoulder. An hour, two passed. Three. My whole body would assume regular movements; my shoveling would be described by identical, even movements. Even later in the day, my enthusiasm for primitive sensation would survive the heat and the dust and the insects pricking my back. I would strain wildly for sensation as the day came to a close. At three-thirty, quitting time, I would stand upright and slowly let my head fall back, luxuriating in the feeling of tightness relieved.

*bracero: A Mexican working as a farm laborer in the United States.

Multiple-Choice Questions

1. In paragraph 1, the author writes, "Desire uncoiled within me."
   He is using

   A. personification.

   B. a simile.

   C. alliteration.

   D. satire.

2. In paragraph 1, what does the word *menial* mean?

   A. enjoyable

   B. lowly

   C. difficult

   D. intellectual

3. In paragraph 5, the author writes, "A nervous spark of pain would fly up my arm and settle to burn like an ember in the thick of my shoulder." This is an example of

   A. symbolism.

   B. onomatopoeia.

   C. metaphor.

   D. flashback.

4. In paragraph 5, what does *luxuriating in* mean?

   A. objecting to

   B. becoming drowsy with

   C. taking delight in

   D. wondering about

5. What is the tone of the last paragraph?

   A. suspicious

   B. enthusiastic

   C. discouraged

   D. worried

6. The author found physical labor to be

   A. boring.

   B. easier than expected.

   C. pleasurable.

   D. annoying.

7. This excerpt is written in which person?

   A. first

   B. second

   C. third

   D. fourth

8. This excerpt is an example of

   A. biography.

   B. myth.

   C. persuasive writing.

   D. autobiography.

Open-Response Question

9. Was the experience of doing physical labor a positive or negative one for the author? Support your answer with specific details from the excerpt.

   _____

   _____

   _____

   _____

   _____

   _____

Reading Selection 2

Read the poem "Mother to Son." Think about what point the poet is making and how he brings that point across. Then answer the questions that follow.

Mother to Son
by Langston Hughes

Well, son, I'll tell you:
Life for me ain't been no crystal stair.
It's had tacks in it,
And splinters,
5 And boards torn up,
And places with no carpet on the floor—
Bare.
But all the time
I'se been a-climbin' on,
10 And reachin' landin's
And turnin' corners
And sometimes goin' in the dark
Where there ain't been no light,
So, boy, don't you turn back.
15 Don't set down on the steps
'Cause you find it kinder hard.
Don't you fall now—
For I'se still goin', honey,
I'se still climbin',
20 And life for me ain't been no crystal stair.

Multiple-Choice Questions

1. The stair in this poem represents

   A. success.

   B. parenthood.

   C. love.

   D. life.

2. Which is **not** used to suggest difficulties that the mother has encountered?

   A. darkness

   B. splinters

   C. doorways

   D. bare places on the floor

3. What is the meaning of the advice given in lines 14-15: "don't you turn back. / Don't set down on the steps"?

   A. Don't give up when life is hard.

   B. Hard work is the key to success.

   C. Don't waste time resting.

   D. Never admit that you're wrong.

4. The mother makes clear to her son that she

   A. has given up.

   B. is leaving.

   C. plans to move to another place.

   D. won't stop trying.

5. What is the main figure of speech used in this poem?

   A. metaphor

   B. personification

   C. hyperbole

   D. allegory

6. What is the tone of this poem?

   A. lighthearted

   B. defeated

   C. encouraging

   D. indifferent

The following short story was written in 1894. As you read, think about the reactions of the main character and what they reveal about the author's theme. When you have finished reading, answer the questions that follow.

The Story of an Hour
by Kate Chopin

1 Knowing that Mrs. Mallard was afflicted with a heart trouble, great care was taken to break to her as gently as possible the news of her husband's death.

2 It was her sister Josephine who told her, in broken sentences, veiled hints that revealed in half concealing. Her husband's friend Richards was there, too, near her. It was he who had been in the newspaper office when intelligence of the railroad disaster was received, with Brently Mallard's name leading the list of "killed." He had only taken the time to assure himself of its truth by a second telegram, and had hastened to forestall any less tender friend in bearing the sad message.

3 She did not hear the story as many women have heard the same, with a paralyzed inability to accept its significance. She wept at once, with sudden, wild abandonment, in her sister's arms. When the storm of grief had spent itself she went away to her room alone. She would have no one follow her.

4 There stood, facing the open window, a comfortable, roomy armchair. Into this she sank, pressed down by a physical exhaustion that haunted her body and seemed to reach into her soul.

5 She could see in the open square before her house the tops of trees that were all aquiver with the new spring life. The delicious breath of rain was in the air. In the street below a peddler was crying his wares. The notes of a distant song which some one was singing reached her faintly, and countless sparrows were twittering in the eaves.

6 There were patches of blue sky showing here and there through the clouds that had met and piled above the other in the west facing her window. She sat with her head thrown back upon the cushion of the chair quite motionless, except when a sob came up into her throat and shook her, as a child who has cried itself to sleep continues to sob in its dreams.

7 She was young, with a fair, calm face, whose lines bespoke repression and even a certain strength. But now there was a dull stare in her eyes, whose gaze was fixed away off yonder on one of those patches of blue sky. It was not a glance of reflection, but rather indicated a suspension of intelligent thought.

8 There was something coming to her and she was waiting for it, fearfully. What was it? She did not know; it was too subtle and elusive to name. But she felt it, creeping out of the sky, reaching toward her through the sounds, the scents, the color that filled the air.

Now her bosom rose and fell tumultuously. She was beginning to recognize this thing that was approaching to possess her, and she was

9 striving to beat it back with her will—as powerless as her two white slender hands would have been.

10 When she abandoned herself a little whispered word escaped her slightly parted lips. She said it over and over under her breath: "Free, free, free!" The vacant stare and the look of terror that had followed it went from her eyes. They stayed keen and bright. Her pulse beat fast, and the coursing blood warmed and relaxed every inch of her body.

11 She did not stop to ask if it were not a monstrous joy that held her. A clear and exalted perception enabled her to dismiss the suggestion as trivial.

12 She knew that she would weep again when she saw the kind, tender hands folded in death; the face that had never looked save with love upon her, fixed and gray and dead. But she saw beyond that bitter moment a long procession of years to come that would belong to her absolutely. And she opened and spread her arms out to them in welcome.

13 There would be no one to live for her during those coming years; she would live for herself. There would be no powerful will bending her in that blind persistence with which men and women believe they have a right to impose a private will upon a fellow creature. A kind intention or a cruel intention made the act seem no less a crime as she looked upon it in that brief moment of illumination.

14 And yet she had loved him—sometimes. Often she had not. What did it matter! What could love, the unsolved mystery, count for in face of this possession of self-assertion which she suddenly recognized as the strongest impulse of her being.

15 "Free! Body and soul free!" she kept whispering.

16 Josephine was kneeling before the closed door with her lips to the keyhole, imploring for admission. "Louise, open the door! I beg; open the door—you will make yourself ill. What are you doing, Louise? For heavens sake open the door."

17 "Go away. I am not making myself ill." No; she was drinking in a very elixir of life through that open window.

18 Her fancy was running riot along those days ahead of her. Spring days, and summer days, and all sorts of days that would be her own. She breathed a quick prayer that life might be long. It was only yesterday she had thought with a shudder that life might be long.

19 She arose at length and opened the door to her sister's importunities. There was a feverish triumph in her eyes, and she carried herself unwittingly like a goddess of Victory. She clasped her sister's waist, and together they descended the stairs. Richards stood waiting for them at the bottom.

20 Some one was opening the front door with a latchkey. It was Brently Mallard who entered, a little travel-stained, composedly carrying his grip-sack and umbrella. He had been far from the scene of accident, and did not even know there had been one. He stood amazed at Josephine's piercing cry; at Richard's quick motion to screen him from the view of his wife.

21 But Richards was too late.

22 When the doctors came they said she had died of heart disease—of joy that kills.

Multiple-Choice Questions

1. In paragraph 8, the author writes, "There was something coming to her..." What was that "something"?

   A. terror at being alone

   B. a feeling of relief

   C. suspicion of her sister

   D. a sense of fairness

2. After her first reaction, Mrs. Mallard realizes that her husband's passing gives her

   A. money.

   B. power.

   C. fame.

   D. freedom.

3. What does paragraph 13 ("There would be no one to live for her...") suggest about Mr. Mallard?

   A. He was a wonderful husband.

   B. He dominated his wife.

   C. He considered himself and his wife equals.

   D. He left important decisions to his wife.

4. Which word is closest to the meaning of *illumination* in paragraph 13?

   A. lighting

   B. understanding

   C. resentment

   D. confusion

5. Mrs. Mallard's initial grief is replaced by

    A. joy.

    B. anger.

    C. amusement.

    D. amazement.

6. This story is an example of

    A. oxymoron.

    B. personification.

    C. irony.

    D. fable.

7. The opening line of the story ("Knowing that Mrs. Mallard was afflicted with a heart trouble...") is an example of

    A. flashback.

    B. metaphor.

    C. foreshadowing.

    D. satire.

Open-Response Question

8. How does Mrs. Mallard's emotional state change during the story? What do these changes suggest about the author's meaning? Use specific evidence from the story to support your answer.

_____

_____

_____

_____

_____

3-7 Understanding Comparison and Contrast

CONCEPTS TO UNDERSTAND

In your daily life, you make all kinds of comparisons. You compare people, places, musical recordings, movies, and many other things.

As a reader, you make comparisons, too. For example, you compare stories, characters, and writing styles. When you read a newspaper, you compare opinions expressed in editorials and letters to the editor.

On the MCAS exam, you'll probably see multiple-choice or open-response questions that involve comparisons in one way or another. Let's examine the basics of comparison and contrast.

- When you compare persons, places, or things, you find similarities between them. For instance, when you compare two cities in Massachusetts, you look for ways the cities are alike.
- When you contrast persons, places, or things, you find differences between them. For example, when you contrast two candidates for governor, you look for ways the candidates are different.
- On the MCAS exam, comparison and contrast may come into play in several ways:

  ~ *As an organizational approach:* The author directly compares two people or places. The comparison may take up just one paragraph, or it may go on for a page or more.
  ~ *As literary elements:* Poets and authors often make comparisons through the use of similes and metaphors, imagery, or symbolism.
  ~ *As a means of analysis:* An open-response question may ask you to compare two short selections.

- Compare and *contrast* have somewhat different meanings. In general use, though, both words imply finding similarities and differences. For instance, to answer an open-response question that asks you to compare two poems, you would usually discuss similarities as well as differences.

Activity P: Learning from Comparisons

Think of two recent instances in which you made a comparison. Maybe you compared two products while shopping. Or maybe you compared the opinions of two friends who were having a disagreement. For each of your examples, answer the following questions.

1. What were you comparing, and why?

Comparison 1:

_____

_____

_____

Comparison 2:

_____

_____

_____

2. On what did you base your comparison? For example, if you were comparing opinions, you probably looked for good reasons to support the opinions.

Comparison 1:

_____

_____

_____

Comparison 2:

_____

_____

_____

3. How did making the comparison prove helpful?

Comparison 1:

_____

_____

_____

Comparison 2:

_____

_____

_____

READING STRATEGIES:
UNDERSTANDING COMPARISON AND CONTRAST

The following strategies will help you zero in on the use of comparison and contrast.

- **Look for comparisons as you read.** Authors make comparisons for a reason. For example, an author may compare health care in 1900 with present-day health care to show how far modern medicine has advanced. A poet may compare a troubled boy to a ship lost at sea to suggest the boy's state of mind.

  When you come across such comparisons, pause to think about them. How are the items compared alike? How are they different? What idea or information is the author trying to get across with the comparison?

- **Watch for words that signal comparisons.** Certain words signal when an author may be comparing or contrasting people, places, or things. Here are some examples.

Words That May Signal Comparison/Contrast	
similar	different
similarity	difference
alike	both
like	as
resembles	opposite
however	on the other hand
but	on the contrary
although	even though

- **Watch for implied comparisons.** Authors communicate a great deal through implied comparisons. Suppose a married couple in a story encounters a homeless man on the street. The husband ignores the man completely, but the wife stops and tries to help him. What might such different reactions suggest about the husband and wife?
- **Understand selections before comparing them.** To compare two selections, first study each selection individually. Be sure you understand each selection's key ideas as well as the author's purpose and point of view. When you feel that you understand both selections, you're ready to identify similarities and differences between them.

TIP: Analogies Make Comparisons

An analogy is a special kind of comparison. Using an analogy, an author compares two items that seem different in order to highlight certain similar features. For example, when science writers explain how the heart is like a pump or the eye is like a camera, they are using analogies.

APPLY YOUR KNOWLEDGE

- The following selection is an excerpt from a short story called "The One Who Goes Farthest Away," about a man who returns to Korea many years after the war. Read the passage and answer the questions. Use the reading strategies that you've learned.
- After you have finished, read the *Think It Through* that follows to see how one student answered the questions.

The One Who Goes Farthest Away

By Katherine Min

1   Thirty-five years ago the street had been dirt, narrow and rutted; there had been stables along it with tired ponies, all their ribs showing through dull, matted coats. Now, as he walked along the red-tiled sidewalk, he watched the cars glide over the smooth black tar, watched the men on bicycles, loaded in back with toilet paper, chickens, and ice, weave in and out of traffic with the intensity of racers.

2   He couldn't help comparing the world he had known with what he now saw; ever since he'd come back, he'd felt this curious simultaneity in his mind, as though the past lay superimposed on the present, playing itself out in phantom traces across the city. Thirty-five years ago there had been oxen to carry the loads, lumbering down the dusty streets attended by thin, indolent men. There had been bicycles too, but not for commerce, ridden by schoolchildren in their starched uniforms who had been freed from the basements of the war.

3   Entering a small courtyard, Kyoungsu marveled at how much the city had changed. The skyscrapers pressed in all around the older, shorter buildings, making them seem not so much like buildings as footstools. When he'd left, the city had been devastated, a dry, gray plain filled with rubble and debris crowded with starving refugees from the North. *Like a *phoenix,* Kyoungsu thought, *the city has rebuilt itself.* He shook his head at the aptness of the image. Out of the ashes.

* phoenix   A mythical bird that is reborn from its own ashes.

1. What comparison does the author make in this passage?

_____

_____

_____

2. Does the comparison show more similarities or differences? Support your answer with specific examples.

_____

_____

_____

3. What is the main point that the author conveys by means of the comparison?

_____

_____

_____

4. In paragraph 3, the author writes that "*Like a phoenix . . . the city has rebuilt itself.*" Explain the meaning of this figure of speech.

_____

_____

_____

Think It Through

1. What comparison does the author make in this passage?

   The author compares the present-day city to the city
   thirty-five years ago.

2. Does the comparison show more similarities or differences? Support your answer with specific examples.

   The comparison is based almost entirely on differences. For
   example, thirty-five years ago there had been a narrow dirt
   street. Now, there is a "red-tiled sidewalk" and a "smooth black
   tar" street. More important, the city Kyoungsu remembers had
   been left in ruins by the war. Now, there is a modern, rebuilt city
   in its place, complete with skyscrapers.

3. What is the main point that the author conveys by means of the comparison?

   By contrasting past and present, the author shows how
   dramatically the city has changed.

4. In paragraph 3, the author writes that "*Like a phoenix . . . the city has rebuilt itself.*" Explain the meaning of this figure of speech.

"Like a phoenix" is a simile. The author is comparing the

rebuilt city to a mythical bird that rose again from its own

ashes. The city, too, rose again, out of the ashes of war.

> *Fill in the blanks:* To compare two selections, first be sure
> that you understand each selection's _____
> as well as the author's
> _____ and _____ .

APPLY YOUR KNOWLEDGE

- Read the following two letters to the editor and answer the questions. Use the reading strategies that you've learned.
- After you have finished, read the *Think It Through* that follows to see how one student answered the questions.

To the Editor:

1. Our town government never seems to run out of projects on which to spend money. In recent years, the town has modernized the library, expanded parking facilities, and planted more trees than anyone can count. However, one project that really does deserve to be funded is a teen center.

2. A teen center would be expensive to build, but it would be worth the cost. First of all, a teen center would give teenagers a fun place to go after school and on weekends, good weather or bad. They could socialize, watch TV, listen to music, and play games. Teens who are too young to drive would especially benefit from having a place to hang out.

3. Second, a teen center could provide a safe haven for teenagers. Despite what some people think, the majority of teens are not hard-drinking, drug-taking vandals. Alcohol and drugs are out there, for sure, but that doesn't mean every teen wants to use them. A teen center would be a place for teenagers <u>not</u> to get into trouble.

4. Let's give the idea serious consideration. We've spent tax dollars on books, cars, and trees. How about spending some on our town's young people?

Sincerely,

Rick Martinez

To the Editor:

Lately, there's been a lot of talk about building a teen center. This is a silly idea.

A teen center would be a complete waste of money. Teenagers just won't go to such a place. A teen center isn't "cool." Teens prefer to spend their time at one another's homes, at the local pizza place, at the park, or at the mall. Besides, teenagers want to feel independent. Most of them would never hang out any place where they're "supposed to" hang out.

Over the past few years, this town has made some much needed improvements. For example, the library has been modernized, and many trees have been planted. There's still much that should be done, though. The town pool needs major work, and some of the ball fields are in sad shape. If there's money to be spent, spend it where it will serve a useful purpose.

Sincerely,

Becca Westfield

1. How does the writer of the first letter support his central point?

_____

_____

_____

2. How does the writer of the second letter support her central point?

_____

_____

_____

3. Compare the two letters. How do they differ? Are there any ways they are alike?

_____

_____

_____

Think It Through

1. How does the writer of the first letter support his central point?

The writer of the first letter thinks that the town should build a teen center. To support this view, the writer explains how such a center would give teens a fun and safe place to hang out.

2. How does the writer of the second letter support her central point?

The writer of the second letter thinks that the town would be wasting its money on a teen center. To support this view, the writer explains why teenagers would not go to such a place.

3. Compare the two letters. How do they differ? Are there any ways they are alike?

The letters differ sharply in point of view. The first letter writer thinks that building a teen center would be a wise use of money. The second letter writer has the opposite viewpoint. She feels that a teen center would be "a complete waste of money."

Both letters mention that the town has spent money modernizing the library and planting trees. Beyond that, the only way in which the two letters are alike is in their basic purpose: to persuade readers how best to spend town money.

REVIEW

Here is a brief summary of what you've learned in section 3-7. To review concepts or strategies in more detail, turn back to the pages indicated.

Concepts to Understand (pages 174-175):

- When you *compare* items, you find similarities between them. When you *contrast* items, you find differences between them. However, in general use, the words *compare* and *comparison* imply finding both *similarities* and *differences*.
- On the MCAS exam, comparison and contrast may come into play in any of several ways: as an organizational approach, as literary elements, or as a means of analysis.

Understanding comparison and contrast (pages 176-177):

- Look for comparisons as you read.
- Watch for words that signal comparisons.
- Watch for implied comparisons.
- Understand selections before comparing them.

PRACTICE

The selections and questions that follow will give you a chance to practice the reading strategies that you've learned in Part 3 and the test-taking strategies that you learned in Part 2. Because MCAS exam questions call for a combination of skills, practice questions touch on skills beyond those covered in just this section.

Read the poem "Caged Bird." Think about how the poet uses symbolism to convey her meaning. Then answer the questions that follow.

Caged Bird
by Maya Angelou

A free bird leaps
on the back of the wind
and floats downstream
till the current ends
5 and dips his wing
in the orange sun ray s
and dares to claim the sky.

But a bird that stalks
down his narrow cage
10 can seldom see through
his bars of rage
his wings are clipped and
his feet are tied
so he opens his throat to sing.

15 The caged bird sings
with a fearful trill
of things unknown
but longed for still
and his tune is heard
20 on the distant hill
for the caged bird
sings of freedom.

The free bird thinks of another breeze
and the trade winds soft through the
   sighing trees
25 and the fat worms waiting on a dawn-
   bright lawn
and he names the sky his own.

But a caged bird stands on the grave
   of dreams
his shadow shouts on a nightmare
   scream
his wings are clipped and his feet are
   tied
30 so he opens his throat to sing.

The caged bird sings
with a fearful trill
of things unknown
but longed for still
35 and his tune is heard
on the distant hill
for the caged bird
sings of freedom.

Multiple-Choice Questions

1. What is the poet's **main** purpose in this poem?

   A. to compare the lives of two birds

   B. to describe how free birds spend their time

   C. to persuade readers that birds should not be caged.

   D. to compare two conditions of the human spirit.

2. The caged bird sings because he

    A. feels happy to be safe.

    B. longs to be free.

    C. misses the company of other birds.

    D. is afraid of the outside world.

3. The imagery in lines 1-7 and lines 23-26 suggests the free bird's

    A. independence.

    B. indecision.

    C. lack of purpose.

    D. calmness.

4. In line 27, what does the poet mean by "a caged bird stands on the grave of dreams"?

    A. The bird is dreaming about death.

    B. The bird cannot dream while inside a cage.

    C. The bird's dreams have died because he cannot pursue them.

    D. The bird's cage is near a graveyard.

Open-Response Question

5. Compare the lives of the caged bird and the free bird. What is the symbolic significance of the differences? Use specific details from the poem to support your answer.

_____

_____

_____

_____

_____

Reading Selections 2A and 2B

The following selections are very different, but they deal with a similar theme. Read the two selections and think about how each author conveys the selection's meaning. Then answer the questions that follow.

SELECTION 2A

The Fighting Roosters and the Eagle

1 In a farmyard lived two Roosters, who bickered night and day. Finally, one afternoon their argument erupted into an all-out battle, beaks pecking and claws tearing. They fought until one Rooster was defeated and limped off to a corner of the farmyard.

2 The victor flew up to the roof of the henhouse. Proudly, he flapped his wings and began crowing as loudly as he could of his mighty triumph. It happened that an Eagle flying overhead heard the Rooster boasting of his victory. In a flash, the Eagle swooped down, snatched up the braggart, and carried him away.

3 Seeing what had happened, the other Rooster emerged from his corner and took over as farmyard master.

"Great pride leads to a great fall."

SELECTION 2B

Arachne

by Olivia Coolidge

1 Arachne[1] was a maiden who became famous throughout Greece, though she was neither noble nor beautiful and came from no great city. She lived in an obscure little village, and her father was a humble dyer of wool. In this he was very skillful, producing many varied shades. Above all he was famous for the clear, bright scarlet, which was made from shellfish and was the most glorious of all the colors used in ancient Greece. Even more skillful than her father was Arachne. It was her task to spin the fleecy wool into a fine, soft thread and to weave it into cloth on the high, standing loom within the cottage. Arachne was small and pale from much working. Her eyes were light, and her hair was a dusty brown; yet she was quick and graceful, and her fingers, roughened as they

---
[1] Greek goddess of wisdom and arts and crafts

were, went so fast that it was hard to follow their flickering movements. So soft and even was her thread, so fine her cloth, so gorgeous her embroidery, that soon her products were known all over Greece. No one had ever seen the like of them before.

2   At last Arachne's fame became so great that people used to come from far and wide to watch her working. Even the graceful nymphs would steal in from stream or forest and peep shyly through the dark doorway, watching in wonder the white arms of Arachne as she stood at the loom and threw the shuttle from hand to hand between the hanging threads, or drew out the long wool, fine as a hair, from the distaff as she sat spinning. "Surely Athene herself must have taught her," people would murmur to one another. "Who else could know the secret of such marvelous skill?"

3   Arachne was used to being wondered at, and she was immensely proud of the skill that had brought so many to look at her. Praise was all she lived for, and it displeased her greatly that people should think anyone, even a goddess, could teach her anything. Therefore, when she heard them murmur, she would stop her work and turn round indignantly to say, "With my own ten fingers, I gained this skill, and by hard practice from early morning till night, I never had time to stand looking, as you people do, while another maiden worked. Nor if I had, would I give Athene credit because the girl was more skillful than I. As for Athene's weaving, how could there be finer cloth or more beautiful embroidery than mine. If Athene herself were to come down and compete with me, she could do no better than I."

4   One day when Arachne turned round with such words, an old woman answered her, a gray old woman, bent and very poor, who stood leaning on a staff and peering at Arachne amid the crowd of onlookers. "Reckless girl," she said. "how dare you claim to be equal to the immortal gods themselves. I am an old woman and have seen much. Take my advice and ask pardon of Athene for your words. Rest content with your fame of being the best spinner and weaver that mortal eyes have ever beheld."

5   "Stupid old woman," said Arachne indignantly, "who gave you a right to speak in this way to me? It is easy to see that you were never good for anything in your day, or you would not have come here in poverty and rags to gaze at my skill. If Athene resents my words, let her answer them herself. I have challenged her to a contest, but she, of course, will not come. It is easy for the gods to avoid matching their skills with that of mortals."

6   At these words the old woman threw down her staff and stood erect. The wondering onlookers saw her grow tall and fair and stand clad in long robes of dazzling white. They were terribly afraid as they realized that they stood in the presence of Athene. Arachne herself flushed red for a moment, for she had never really believed that the goddess would hear her. Before the group that was gathered there, she would not give in; so, pressing her pale lips together in obstinacy and pride, she led the goddess to one of her great looms and set herself before the other. Without a word, both began to thread the long woolen strands that hung from the rollers and between which the shuttle moved back and forth. Many skeins lay heaped beside them to use, bleached white, and gold, and scarlet, and other shades, varied as the rainbow. Arachne had never thought of giving credit for her success to her father's skill in dyeing, though in actual truth the colors were as remarkable as the cloth itself.

7 Soon there was no sound in the room but the breathing of the onlookers, the whirring of the shuttles, and the creaking of the wooden frames as each weaver pressed the thread up into place or tightened the pegs by which the whole was held straight. The excited crowd in the doorway began to see that the skill of both in truth was very nearly equal, but that however the cloth might turn out, the goddess was the quicker of the two. A pattern of many pictures was growing on her loom. There was a border of twined branches of the olive, Athene's favorite tree, while in the middle, figures began to appear. As they looked at the glowing colors, the spectators realized that Athene was weaving into her pattern a last warning to Arachne. The central figure was the goddess herself competing with Poseidon[2] for possession of the city of Athens; but in the four corners were mortals who had tried to strive with gods and pictures of the awful fate that had overtaken them. The goddess ended a little before Arachne and stood back from her marvelous work to see what the maiden was doing.

8 Never before had Arachne been matched against anyone whose skill was equal, or even nearly equal, to her own. As she stole glances from time to time at Athene and saw the goddess working swiftly, calmly, and always a little faster than herself, she became angry instead of frightened—and an evil thought, came into her head. Thus, as Athene stepped back a pace to watch Arachne finishing her work, she saw that the maiden had taken for her design a pattern of scenes that showed evil or unworthly actions of the gods, how they had resorted to trickery and had appeared on earth from time to time in the form of poor and humble people. When the goddess saw this insult glowing in bright colors on Arachne's loom, she did not wait while the cloth was judged, but stepped forward, her gray eyes blazing with anger, and tore Arachne's work across.

9 "Wicked girl," she said. "Live on and spin, both you and your descendants. When people look at you, they may remember that it is not wise to strive with Athene." At that, the body of Arachne shriveled up, and her legs grew tiny and spindly. There before the eyes of the spectators hung a little dusty brown spider on a slender thread.

10 All spiders descend from Arachne: and any time that the Greeks watched them spinning their thread wonderfully fine, they remembered the contest with Athene and thought that it was not right for even the best of mortals to claim equality with the gods.

Multiple-Choice Questions

1. In line 1 of "The Fighting Roosters and the Eagle," what does the word *bickered* mean?

   A. guarded

   B. chatted

   C. quarreled

   D. crowed

---

2 Greek god of the sea

2. In paragraph 6 of "Arachne," what does the word *obstinacy* mean?

    A. fear

    B. stubbornness

    C. enthusiasm

    D. sadness

3. Arachne can best be described as

    A. cautious.

    B. respectful.

    C. humble.

    D. conceited.

4. In both selections, a character

    A. causes his or her own downfall.

    B. disregards a warning.

    C. grows wiser from experience.

    D. defeats a stronger opponent.

5. Both selections contain a message about

    A. fighting.

    B. loyalty.

    C. pride.

    D. deceit.

6. Which of the following is true?

    A. Both selections are fables.

    B. Both selections are myths.

    C. "The Fighting Roosters and the Eagle" is an allegory; "Arachne" is a satire.

    D. "The Fighting Roosters and the Eagle" is a fable; "Arachne" is a myth.

Open-Response Question

7. Explain how "The Fighting Roosters and the Eagle" and
    "Arachne" present a similar message in different ways. Use
    details from both selections to support your answer.

    _____

    _____

    _____

    _____

    _____

    _____

3-8 Answering Other Kinds of Questions

CONCEPTS AND STRATEGIES

Part 3 has focused on the key reading and thinking skills needed for the MCAS exam. However, the Language and Literature portion of the exam also touches on some other areas of English. For instance, you may find questions that test your knowledge of grammar or your understanding of the English language.

There isn't enough space in this book to review every aspect of language arts. However, in the following pages, we'll briefly examine some examples of other kinds of questions that may appear on the exam.

If any of the terms or concepts discussed in this section are new or unclear to you, check your textbook or ask your teacher for help.

TIP: Take Time to Help Yourself

You probably have a good sense of your strengths and weaknesses. Maybe you organize your thoughts well, but your grammar could be better. Or maybe you have a large vocabulary, but your writing is not as clear as it should be.

Help yourself! Look back at your English papers and identify areas that need improvement. Work on those areas. Review your textbooks. Do practice activities. Ask your teacher for helpful suggestions.

If you come upon a sample exam question that puzzles you, find out how to answer such a question. It is better to learn what you need to know now, before the exam, than to look back afterward and say, "if only I had learned that . . ."

Grammar and Usage Questions

The Language and Literature portion of the MCAS exam often includes a few grammar and usage questions. For example, you may see questions that look like this:

What is the subject of the verb *give* in the first sentence in paragraph 3?

A. poets

B. you

C. pens

D. thoughts

What is the main clause of the second sentence in paragraph 2?

A. " . . . builds her dreams of the future."

B. " . . . a home, which everyone treasures."

C. " . . . the vision clearest in her mind . . . "

D. "In a private moment . . . "

To prepare for grammar and usage questions, you may want to review such basics as:

- types of clauses
- types of phrases
- verb forms and tenses
- pronouns and antecedents
- sentence structure

Activity Q: Reviewing a Few Grammar Basics

Answer the following questions. If you need help, consult a grammar book.

  1. What is the difference between a main clause and a subordinate clause?

_____

_____

_____

2. Write a sentence containing both a main clause and a subordinate clause.

_____

_____

_____

3. Identify the subject and verb in the sentence you wrote.

_____

_____

_____

Language-Related Questions

The exam often includes at least a question or two dealing with language. Here are two examples:

Example 1: Mrs. Tropp asks, "You want I should take you now to hospital?" The language she uses can best be described as

    A. slang.

    B. formal English.

    C. jargon.

    D. dialect.

Example 2: Lines 23-27 are an example of

    A. standard English.

    B. slang.

    C. dialect.

    D. non-standard English.

To prepare for such questions about language, you should know the differences between standard and nonstandard American English. You should also know what _dialect, slang,_ and _jargon_ are and be able to identify examples of each.

Questions About Words

Questions about the meaning of words often appear on the MCAS exam. Usually you can use context clues to help you answer these questions.

There may also be a question about the origin—or etymology—of a word, accompanied by a dictionary entry. Here's an example:

> **in·spire** \in-'spir\ vb **in·spired; inspiring** [ME, fr. MF & L: MF *inspirer,* fr. L *inspirare,* fr. *in-* + *spirare* to breath] *vt* (14c) **1 a:** to influence, move or guide by divine or supernatural inspiration **b:** to exert an animating, enlivening, or exalting influence on ⟨was particularly *inspired* by the Romanticists⟩ **c:** to spur on: IMPEL, MOTIVATE ⟨threats don't necessarily ~ people to work⟩ **d:** AFFECT ⟨seeing the old room again *inspired* him with nostalgia⟩ **2 a:** archaic: to breathe

According to the dictionary entry, the word *inspire* originated in what language?

A. French

B. Arabic

C. Latin

D. Greek

To prepare for questions about words, review section 3-4, *Using Context Clues to Determine Meaning* (pages 114-130). You should also work to develop your vocabulary: see the suggestions in the box on page 18, Tip: Build Your Vocabulary.

If you don't fully understand all the parts of dictionary entries, ask your teacher for help. Being able to use a dictionary is an essential skill for reading and writing.

TIP: Become Familiar with Dictionary Abbreviations

Learn the most common abbreviations used in dictionary entries. For example, you should know how the dictionary abbreviates parts of speech. You should also understand the abbreviations that appear in etymologies, such as *L* or *Lat* for Latin and *ME* for Middle English.

Questions About Sequence

Sometimes the MCAS exam includes questions about *sequence* or *sequential order*—the order in which things happen or are organized. For example, an informational article may list a sequence of steps required to perform a task, such as baking a cake. The steps must be carried out in the proper order to complete the task.

Here are two examples of questions about sequence. Both questions refer to a reading passage about a bike trip across the country.

After leaving Massachusetts, what two states did the bikers travel through next?

A. New York, then Pennsylvania

B. New York, then New Jersey

C. Connecticut, then New York

D. Connecticut, then Pennsylvania

If the bikers were to return to Massachusetts by reversing the order of states they passed through, what state would they cross after Nevada?

A. California

B. Utah

C. Idaho

D. Colorado

Note that certain words may signal sequential order. Here are some examples:

Words That May Signal Sequential Order

after	before	first, second, etc.
afterward	last	later
next	then	subsequently
yesterday	today	tomorrow

To prepare for questions about sequence, review the various ways authors organize information. For example, the author of a historical novel may describe events in the order in which they took place. An essay writer may present ideas and supporting details in order from the least important to the most important so as to build to a conclusion.

Complete the sentence: The order in which things happen or are organized is known as _____.

TIP: Authors Often Use Chronological Order

The most common sequence is chronological. Using this form of organization, authors present events or information in time order, usually moving forward in time.

The word chronological comes from the Greek word chronos, which means "time."

APPLY YOUR KNOWLEDGE

- The following selection is an excerpt from a short story. Read the passage and answer the questions. Use the reading strategies that you've learned.
- After you have finished, read the *Think It Through* that follows to see how one student answered the questions.

Travels with Andy

1   As Andy and I drove west from Jackson along Route 301, the morning sun vanished behind dark gray clouds. The temperature began to drop, and wind gusts buffeted the car.

2   "Rock and roll!" my little brother laughed, as the car swayed.

3   We stayed on Route 301 for eighteen miles, passing ugly factory towns and polluted lakes. Then we turned north and headed toward Redmont along Route 5. The scenery along this road was gorgeous: rugged mountains covered with tall trees. Andy was amazed, as though he'd never been out of the city before. "Cool!" he said about a hundred times.

4   We'd traveled another fifteen more miles or so, passing first through Lakeville and then Monroe, when the storm hit. The rain came down lightly at first, then more and more heavily, until finally the deluge forced us to pull over somewhere near Danburgh. "Cool!" Andy said again, as he watched the rain gush down over the windshield like a waterfall. I was less impressed. For me, the storm was just an inconvenience.

5   We were stuck for nearly an hour before the downpour slowed enough for us to resume our trip. By the time we reached Redmont, the rain had stopped completely. In fact, the sun was now shining brightly, and the sky had turned bright blue. Andy lowered his window, and let the wind blow through his hair. He grinned at me.

6   "Don't say it," I started, but I wasn't quick enough.

7   "*Cool!*" Andy said with a chuckle.

1. In paragraph 1, what does the word *buffeted* mean?

   A. beat against

   B. cooled

   C. cleaned off

   D. moistened

2. As the travelers moved from Route 301 to Route 5, their surroundings

   A. became less pleasant.

   B. became more pleasant.

   C. changed only very little.

   D. did not change at all.

3. In paragraph 4, what does the word *deluge* mean?

   A. police

   B. dense fog

   C. darkness

   D. heavy rainfall

   re·sume \ri-'züm/ *vb* **re·sumed; re·sum·ing** [ME, fr. MF or L; MF *resumer,* fr. L *resumere,* fr. *re-* + *sumere* to take up, take — more at CONSUME] *vt* (15c) **1:** to assume or take again: REOCCUPY ⟨*resumed* his seat by the fire—Thomas Hardy⟩ **2:** to return to or begin again after interruption ⟨*resumed* her work⟩ **3:** to take back to oneself **4:** to pick up again **5:** REITERATE, SUMMARIZE ∼ *vi* : to begin again something interrupted

4. According to the dictionary entry, the word *resume* originated in what language?

   A. French

   B. German

   C. Latin

   D. Greek

5. In paragraph 5, "By the time we reached Redmont," is

   A. a subordinate clause.

   B. a main clause.

   C. a participle.

   D. an infinitive.

6. If the travelers returned to Jackson by following exactly the same route in reverse, they would

    A. pass through Danburgh last.

    B. pass through Redmont, then Lakeville.

    C. reach Lakeville before Monroe.

    D. drive through Lakeville after Monroe.

7. Andy's use of the word *cool* is an example of

    A. formal language.

    B. slang.

    C. jargon.

    D. standard English.

Think It Through

1. In paragraph 1, what does the word *buffeted* mean?

    A. beat against

    B. cooled

    C. cleaned off

    D. moistened

Context clues tell me that choice A is correct. Wind gusts made the car sway, so the wind must be beating against the car.

2. As the travelers moved from Route 301 to Route 5, their surroundings

    A. became less pleasant.

    B. became more pleasant.

    C. changed only very little.

    D. did not change at all.

After "passing ugly factory towns and polluted lakes" on 301, the scenery along Route 5 "was gorgeous." The correct answer is choice B.

3. In paragraph 4, what does the word *deluge* mean?

    A. police

    B. dense fog

    C. darkness

    D. heavy rainfall

Only choice D is specifically supported by the context, so it must be correct.

4. According to the dictionary entry above, the word *resume* originated in which language?

    A. French

    B. German

    C. Latin

    D. Greek

Choice C is correct. Resume can be traced back to Latin, through Middle English and Middle French.

5. In paragraph 5, "By the time we reached Redmont," is

    A. a subordinate clause.

    B. a main clause.

    C. a participle.

    D. an infinitive.

"By the time we reached Redmont" is a subordinate clause. The main clause in the sentence is "the rain had stopped completely." Participles and infinitives are verb forms, not sentence parts. The correct answer is choice A.

6. If the travelers returned to Jackson by following exactly the same route in reverse, they would

    A. pass through Danburgh last.

    B. pass through Redmont, then Lakeville.

    C. reach Lakeville before Monroe.

    D. drive through Lakeville after Monroe.

Reversing their sequence, the travelers would drive first through Monroe and then Lakeville. Choice D is correct.

7. Andy's use of the word *cool* is an example of

    A. formal language.

    B. slang.

    C. jargon.

    D. standard English.

The word cool as Andy uses it is slang. Choice B is correct.

REVIEW

Here is a brief summary of what you've learned in section 3-8.

- To prepare for grammar and usage questions, review such basics as types of clauses and phrases, verb forms and tenses, pronouns and antecedents, and sentence structure.
- To prepare for questions about language, review the differences between standard and nonstandard American English. You should also understand, and be able to recognize, dialect, slang, and jargon.
- To prepare for questions about words, review section 3-4, *Using Context Clues to Determine Meaning* (pages 114-130). Also, if you don't understand all the parts of dictionary entries, ask your teacher for help.
- To prepare for questions about sequence or sequential order, review the ways authors organize information. Also watch for words that signal sequential order.

PRACTICE

The selections and questions that follow will give you a chance to practice the reading strategies that you've learned in Part 3 and the test-taking strategies that you learned in Part 2. Because MCAS exam questions call for a combination of skills, practice questions touch on skills beyond those covered in just this section.

Reading Selection 1

The following selection traces the history of the American cowboy. Read the selection and then answer the questions that follow.

The American Cowboy

1 No figure in American history has been as integral to myth, legend, and romance as the American cowboy. The story of this lone figure, rugged and free, has been sung, told, written, filmed, and painted. The image of the rough-and-ready cowboy, with his horse for company and his cattle to protect, has captured the hearts of the American people. The reality of the cowboy's experience, however, was often quite different from the myth.

2 Cattle were introduced to the New World by the Spanish in the seventeenth century. The first cowboys were actually Mexicans, who were trained by Spanish cattlemen, or *vaqueros.* The Spanish tradition still lingers in the language of the cowboy trade. The lariat, used for roping cattle, comes from the Spanish *la reata.* The heavy leather leggings, or chaps, that cowboys wore to protect their breeches came from the Spanish *chapparal,* and the ponies' bridles were called "hackamores," from the Spanish *jaquima.* The Spanish left their mark on the cowboy's clothing as well. High-heeled durable leather boots, designed to slip easily into stirrups, were worn by the Spanish *vaqueros* long before "cowboy boots" came into vogue. The bandanna, a multi-purpose scrap of cloth, was also worn by *vaqueros.* Later, cowboys found that the bandanna could be used for a handkerchief, a sling, a lunch holder, or a face mask to protect them from the dust raised by thousands of hooves beating on dry ground.

3 The original cowboys had a fairly low-key job. They stayed primarily on the large Spanish-style ranches that flourished throughout Texas and much of the Southwest. The real heyday of the cowboy, however, began shortly after the Civil War. Cowboys were needed to drive the cattle from Texas to railheads in the Midwest, where the cattle were loaded onto trains and shipped to Kansas City, Chicago, and St. Louis. Although the legend of the lonesome cowboy seems as old as America, the actual period of cowboys on the trail was only about 20 years, from the 1860s to the 1880s.

4   The cowboys who rode the ranges during those 20 years were the ones who left their mark on American history and mythology. They came from all over the country, particularly the South where young single men were looking for work. Many black Americans found opportunity and acceptance on the open range. The Western ranches were one of the few places after the Civil War where hiring was based on the ability to perform the job well rather than on skin color or family origin.

5   The cowboy's work began in the spring. The first job was to round up the cattle and herd them into pens. The cattle were then separated by their brands, the marks burned into their sides by hot irons. Young calves had to be branded with the same symbol as their mothers. Each ranch in Texas has its own distinctive brand registered with the Cattleman's Association. Unbranded cattle could be claimed and branded by any rancher who found them. An enterprising cowboy named Sam Maverick built so many herds this way that unbranded cattle became known as "mavericks."

6   After roundup and branding, the cowboys saddled up their ponies and hit the trail. Small herds of about 1,000 cattle could be handled by four or five cowhands, but they often joined larger groups and traveled together. The cattle were driven as much as 1,500 miles through the open range, a journey that could take several months. Cowboys were not paid until they reached the railhead, and they were known for their wild celebrations at the end of the trail. Some of the more ambitious cowboys took their pay in cattle and became ranchers themselves.

7   The days of the open ranges came to an abrupt end in the 1890s. The introduction of barbed wire was largely responsible for the change. Farmers were able to fence in their cattle, and the vast expanses of open land and trails came to an end. The expansion of the railroad enabled ranchers to simply load their herds of cattle directly onto the train, which ended the need for cattle trails. New farming methods involving irrigation also contributed to the demise of the cowboy as we know him.

8   Being a cowboy is a vastly different job today than it was 100 years ago. It is primarily a ranch job now, not a wilderness trek. While the ranches can be so enormous that they are measured in units of RI's (Rhodes Islands), they have become more mechanized, and many of the cowboys' skills have become obsolete. Cowboys continue to stay in touch with their heritage, however, through the rodeo shows that are popular throughout the United States. And cowboy outfits continue to be stylish and comfortable, giving great pleasure to the "drugstore" cowboys among us.

Multiple-Choice Questions

1. The word *lariat* is an example of

    A. a Spanish word.

    B. a word derived from Spanish.

    C. slang spoken by American cowboys.

    D. Western dialect.

2. What is the main clause of the last sentence in paragraph 3?

   A. " . . . the actual period of cowboys on the trail was only about 20 years . . . "

   B. " . . . from the 1860s to the 1880s."

   C. " . . . seems as old as America . . . "

   D. "Although the legend of the lonesome cowboy seems as old as America . . . "

3. After rounding up the cattle, the next step was to

   A. brand them.

   B. drive them to the railhead.

   C. fence them in with barbed wire.

   D. put them into pens.

4. Which of the following was **not** a factor that contributed to the end of the cowboy era?

   A. the development of new farming methods

   B. the use of barbed wire

   C. the introduction of the cattle drive

   D. the expansion of the railroad

   1ro·deo /ˈrō-de-ō, rə-ˈdā(ˌ)ō/ *n, pl* **ro·de·os** [Sp, fr. *rodear* to surround, fr. *rueda* wheel, fr. L *rota*—more at ROLL] (1834) **1:** ROUNDUP **2 a:** a public performance featuring bronco riding, calf roping, steer wrestling, and Brahma bull riding   **b:** a contest resembling a rodeo

5. The dictionary entry above shows that the word *rodeo* originated in

   A. English.

   B. Latin.

   C. Spanish.

   D. French.

6. According to the selection, the popular view of the American cowboy was most shaped by

   A. Mexican cowboys.

   B. Spanish *vaqueros*.

   C. cowboys living after the 1890s.

   D. cowboys living from the 1860s to the 1880s.

The following excerpt is from an essay titled "You're Short Besides!" Read the excerpt and answer the questions that follow.

You're Short Besides!

by Sucheng Chan

1 When asked to write about being a physically handicapped Asian American woman, I considered it an insult. After all, my accomplishments are many, yet I was not asked to write about any of them. Is being handicapped the most salient feature about me? The fact that it might be in the eyes of others made me decide to write the essay as requested. I realized that the way I think about myself may differ considerably from the way others perceive me. And maybe that's what being physically handicapped is all about.

2 I was stricken simultaneously with pneumonia and polio at the age of four. Uncertain whether I had polio of the lungs, seven of the eight doctors who attended me—all practitioners of Western medicine—told my parents they should not feel optimistic about my survival. A Chinese fortune teller my mother consulted also gave a grim prognosis, but for an entirely different reason: I had been stricken because my name was offensive to the gods. My grandmother had named me "grandchild of wisdom," a name that the fortune teller said was too presumptuous for a girl. So he advised my parents to change my name to "chaste virgin." All these pessimistic predictions notwithstanding I hung onto life, if only by a thread. For three years, my body was periodically pierced with electric shocks as the muscles of my legs atrophied. Before my illness, I had been an active, rambunctious, precocious, and very curious child. Being confined to bed was thus a mental agony as great as my physical pain. Living in war-torn China, I received little medical attention; physical therapy was unheard of. But I was determined to walk. So one day, when I was six or seven, I instructed my mother to set up two rows of chairs to face each other so that I could use them as I would parallel bars. I attempted to walk by holding my body up and moving it forward with my arms while dragging my legs along behind. Each time I fell, my mother gasped, but I badgered her until she let me try again. After four nonambulatory years, I finally walked once more by pressing my hands against my thighs so my knees wouldn't buckle.

3 My father had been away from home during most of those years because of the war. When he returned, I had to confront the guilt he felt about my condition. In many East Asian cultures, there is a strong folk belief that a person's physical state in this life is a reflection of how morally or sinfully he or she lived in previous lives. Furthermore, because of the tendency to view the family as a single unit, it is believed that the fate of one member can be caused by the behavior of another. Some of my father's relatives told him that my illness had doubtless been caused by the wild carousing he did in his youth. A well-meaning but somewhat simple man, my father believed them.

4 Throughout my childhood, he sometimes apologized to me for having to suffer retribution for his former bad behavior. This upset me; it was bad enough that I had to deal with the anguish of not being able to walk, but to have to assuage his guilt as well was a real burden! In other ways, my father was very good to me. He took me out often, carrying me on his shoulders or back, to give me fresh air and sunshine. He did this until I was too large and heavy for him to carry. And ever since I can remember, he has told me that I am pretty.

5 After getting over her anxieties about my constant falls, my mother decided to send me to school. I had already learned to read some words of Chinese at the age of three by asking my parents to teach me the sounds and meaning of various characters in the daily newspaper. But between the ages of four and eight, I received no education since just staying alive was a full-time job. Much to her chagrin, my mother found no school in Shanghai, where we lived at the time, which would accept me as a student. Finally, as a last resort, she approached the American School, which agreed to enroll me only if my family kept an *amah* (a servant who takes care of children) by my side at all times. The tuition at the school was twenty U.S. dollars per month—a huge sum of money during those years of runaway inflation in China—and payable only in U.S. dollars. My family afforded the high cost of tuition and the expense of employing a full-time *amah* for less than a year.

6 We left China as the Communist forces swept across the country in victory. We found an apartment in Hong Kong across the street from a school run by Seventh-Day Adventists. By that time I could walk a little, so the principal was persuaded to accept me. An *amah* now had to take care of me only during recess when my classmates might easily knock me over as they ran about the playgrounds.

7 After a year and a half in Hong Kong, we moved to Malaysia, where my father's family had lived for four generations. There I learned to swim in the lovely warm waters of the tropics and fell in love with the sea. On land I was a cripple; in the ocean I could move with the grace of a fish. I liked the freedom of being in the water so much that many years later, when I was a graduate student in Hawaii, I became greatly enamored with a man just because he called me a "Polynesian water nymph."

8 As my overall health improved, my mother became less anxious about all aspects of my life. She did everything possible to enable me to lead as normal a life as possible. I remember how once some of her colleagues in the high school where she taught criticized her for letting me wear short skirts. They felt my legs should not be exposed to public view. My mother's response was, "All girls her age wear short skirts, so why shouldn't she?"

9 The years in Malaysia were the happiest of my childhood, even though I was constantly fending off children who ran after me calling, "*Baikah! Baikah!*" ("Cripple! Cripple!" in the Hokkien dialect commonly spoken in Malaysia). The taunts of children mattered little because I was a star pupil. I won one award after another for general scholarship as well as for art and public speaking. Whenever the school had important visitors my teacher always called on me to recite in front of the class.

A significant event that marked me indelibly occurred when I was twelve. That year my school held a music recital and I was one of the students chosen to play the piano. I managed to get up the steps to the stage without any problem, but as I walked across the stage, I fell. Out of the audience, a voice said loudly and clearly, "Ayah! A *baikah* shouldn't be allowed to perform in public." I got up before anyone could get on

10   stage to help me and, with tears streaming uncontrollably down my face, I rushed to the piano and began to play. Beethoven's "Für Elise" had never been played so fiendishly fast before or since, but I managed to finish the whole piece. That I managed to do so made me feel really strong. I never again feared ridicule.

Multiple-Choice Questions

1. This excerpt is an example of

   A. satire.

   B. allegory.

   C. autobiography.

   D. biography.

2. The organization of information in this essay is

   A. geographical.

   B. chronological.

   C. hierarchical.

   D. spatial.

3. In the first sentence of paragraph 2, stricken is an example of

   A. a present participle.

   B. a past participle.

   C. past tense of a verb.

   D. an infinitive.

at·ro·phy \\'a-trə-fe\\ *n, pl* **-phies** [**LL** *atrophia,* Gk, fr. *atrophos,* ill fed, fr. *a- + trephein* to nourish] (1601) **1:** decrease in size or wasting away of a body part or tissue; *also:* arrested development or loss of a part or organ incidental to the normal development or life of an animal or plant **2:** a wasting away or progressive decline: DEGENERATION ⟨the ~ of freedom⟩ ⟨was not a solitude of ~, of negation, but of perpetual flowering—Willa Cather⟩ — **atrophic** \\ (,)a-'tro-fik\ *adj* —**atrophy** /a-trə-fē, - ,fī*vb*

4. According to the dictionary entry above, the word *atrophy* originated in which language?

   A. Latin

   B. French

   C. Greek

   D. German

5. In paragraph 4, what does the word *retribution* mean?

   A. punishment

   B. disability

   C. hardship

   D. reward

6. The word *baikah* is an example of

   A. slang.

   B. non-standard English.

   C. dialect.

   D. jargon.

7. The author's account suggests that she wants other people to

   A. remember that her father was to blame for her illness.

   B. focus on her accomplishments rather than her limitations.

   C. pay more attention to the fact that she is Asian American.

   D. give her special privileges because of her physical handicap.

8. In the last paragraph, why does the author consider the incident a "significant event that marked me indelibly"?

    A. Everyone was amazed at how fast she could play the piano.

    B. She proved that she had musical talent.

    C. She had never before appeared before an audience.

    D. The event strengthened her self-confidence.

Open-Response Question

9. In the first paragraph, the author writes: " . . . the way I think about myself may differ considerably from the way others perceive me. And maybe that's what being physically handicapped is all about." Using information from the excerpt, explain what she means.

_____

_____

_____

_____

_____

_____

PART FOUR

MCAS Composition: Writing an Essay

> **4-1** Understanding the Writing Task
> **4-2** Carrying out the Writing Task

"The secret of all good writing is sound judgment."

The Roman poet Horace wrote these words more than 2,000 years ago. Horace's "secret" is one you probably already knew. Good writing doesn't just happen. It requires careful thinking and planning.

This part of the book will help you prepare for the Composition portion of the MCAS English Language Arts exam. You'll develop your ability to plan and write an essay in response to a prompt.

The Composition portion of the MCAS English Language Arts exam is designed to test your writing skills. You'll be asked to write a clearly developed, well-organized essay relating either to a work of literature that you've read or to a given reading passage.

In Part 4, you will learn to plan, write, revise, and edit an essay for the Composition portion of the MCAS exam. Some of the points covered may already be familiar to you from class writing assignments. In addition, you will learn strategies to help you respond to different kinds of Composition prompts.

4-1 Understanding the Writing Task

THE COMPOSITION PROMPT

Unlike the Language and Literature part of the exam, the Composition portion contains no multiple-choice questions. Instead, you'll be asked to write an essay based on a prompt. The prompt may take various forms, and it may or may not include a brief reading passage.

You will have approximately two periods to write your essay, scheduled on the same day, with a break in between. Generally, the first period is for planning and writing the first draft of your essay. The second period is for revising and editing your draft.

Scoring Guidelines

Your essay will be scored for topic development and use of writing conventions. Specifically, readers will evaluate your work for the following elements:

DEVELOPMENT	CONVENTIONS
Development of ideas	Sentence structure
Organization	Grammar and word usage
Supporting details	Spelling, capitalization, punctuation
Language and style	

Keep in mind that these elements are all parts of a whole. In other words, to create an effective written work, you need to pay attention to the various elements that come together to form that work. This is true not just when you write an exam essay, but for any kind of writing that you do.

Kinds of Prompts

The writing prompt for the Composition portion of the exam may be constructed around a brief reading passage or around a "critical lens."

A critical lens is a statement or a quotation that you use to analyze a work of literature. Let's look at an example of each kind of prompt.

Study the two sample writing prompts that follow. Think carefully about how the prompts are alike and how they differ.

Sample Writing Prompt 1: With Reading Passage

Read the following opening paragraphs from a short story by Jack London. When you have finished reading, respond to the writing assignment that follows.

To Build a Fire
By Jack London

For land travel or seafaring, the world over, a companion is usually considered desirable. In the Klondike, as Tom Vincent found out, such a companion is absolutely essential. But he found it out, not by precept, but through bitter experience.

"Never travel alone," is a precept of the north. He had heard it many times and laughed; for he was a strapping young fellow, big-boned and big-muscled, with faith in himself and in the strength of his head and hands.

It was on a bleak January day when the experience came that taught him respect for the frost, and for the wisdom of the men who had battled with it.

He had left Calumet Camp on the Yukon with a light pack on his back, to go up Paul Creek to the divide between it and Cherry Creek, where his party was prospecting and hunting moose.

The frost was sixty degree below zero, and he had thirty miles of lonely trail to cover, but he did not mind. In fact, he enjoyed it, swinging along through the silence, his blood pounding warmly through his veins, and his mind carefree and happy. For he and his comrades were certain they had struck "pay" up there on the Cherry Creek Divide; and, further, he was returning to them from Dawson with cheery home letters from the States.

Assignment:

In many literary works, the opening paragraphs offer clues to events that follow. Read the above paragraphs for such clues. Based on these clues, write an essay discussing what might happen in this story. In developing your essay, think about the significance of the first paragraph and consider such elements of the passage as word choice, point of view, tone, mood, setting, and characters.

Sample Writing Prompt 2: With "Critical Lens" Statement

In literature, as in life, people pursue love, truth, happiness, or power. Sometimes they succeed in their quest, sometimes not.

Assignment:

Identify a work of literature that you have read in or out of class that illustrates this statement. Write an essay in which you describe a character's pursuit of "love, truth, happiness, or power." Explain whether or not the character succeeded in his or her quest and why.

Both prompts ask you to write an essay relating to a literary work. For Sample 1, your essay would be based on the reading passage taken from the Jack London short story.

For Sample 2, you would base your essay on "a work of literature that you have read in or out of class." To write this essay, you would use the critical lens statement: "In literature, as in life, people pursue love, truth, happiness, or power. Sometimes they succeed in their quest, sometimes not."

TIP: Look Through the "Lens"

A lens is something you look through in order to see. The term critical lens is used to suggest a way of "seeing" literature critically. In this sense, the statement or quotation included in a Composition prompt is meant to guide your analysis of a work of literature and provide a specific framework for your essay.

Activity A: Comparing Prompts

In your own words, describe the similarities in and differences between a prompt based on a reading passage and a prompt based on a critical lens statement.

_____

_____

_____

RESPONDING TO A SPECIFIC PROMPT

To write your essay, you'll have to tailor your approach to the particular prompt. Since you don't know which form of prompt may appear on the exam, you have to be ready to respond to both.

The following strategies fall into three groups:

- strategies to use for any prompt
- strategies for a prompt with a reading passage
- strategies for a prompt with a critical lens statement

Strategies: Any Composition Prompt

- **Read the prompt carefully.** Be sure you understand exactly what you're being asked to do.
- **Look for key words and phrases.** Just as in Language and Literature questions, key words in a Composition prompt are often verbs, such as *explain, describe,* or *analyze*. Such words help to define or clarify the writing task.

Other words besides verbs also help to define the task. For example, in Sample Writing Prompt 1 (page 211), key words and phrases include clues as well as word *choice, point of view, tone, mood, setting,* and *characters*. In Sample Writing Prompt 2 (page 212), key words include *love, truth, happiness, power,* and *quest*.

To stay focused on what's important, you may find it helpful to <u>underline</u> the key words and phrases in the prompt.

Strategies: Prompt with Reading Passage

- **Read the passage at least twice.** Think carefully about the passage and how it relates to the prompt. Look for stated and implied main ideas. Use the various reading and thinking skills that you learned in Part 3 of this book to help you analyze what you read.
- **Think about elements and techniques.** Consider characters, imagery, point of view, and other elements. Think about why these elements are important in the passage and how they may relate to the prompt.
- **Jot down notes.** As discussed in Part 2, writing down important points can help you understand what you read. In addition, you can tailor your notes to the particular prompt. For example, if the prompt refers to setting, you note references to setting in the passage.

To review suggestions for taking notes, refer back to
Note-Taking Tips, pages 18-20 of Part 2.

Fill in the blank: A critical lens is a statement or a quotation
that you use to _____ a work of literature.

Strategies: Prompt with Critical Lens Statement

- **Consider ahead of time which works of literature you might write about.** Of course, you can't know in advance what the critical lens statement might be. However, most works of literature that you read for school will prove suitable for a wide range of critical lens statements.
- **Be ready to write about more than one book.** The more works of literature you've read and can write about, the more you'll have to choose from. If you know only one book well, and it doesn't relate to the critical lens statement, you could be stuck for something to write about. Therefore, try to be prepared with at least two or three different works.

Be sure you thoroughly understand the content and meaning of books that you may want to discuss. Take time to review the books before the exam. You'll find it helpful to take notes—or to study notes previously taken for school. Allow extra review time for books that are no longer fresh in your mind.

- **Choose substantial works.** The richer the books you've read, the more substance you'll have to work with. Also, the richer the books, the more critical lens statements they are likely to "connect" with.

Activity B: Choosing Works of Literature

1. List below the titles and authors of at least two substantial works of literature you've read that you feel you know well enough to use for the exam.

_____

_____

_____

2. Next to each work that you listed, note how much study and review you'll need to do before the exam. Use the following system of one, two, or three stars to indicate the level of review needed:

*	I read this book very recently. It's still fresh in my mind. I'll just need to look back over my notes.
* *	It's been a while since I read this book. Although I remember it fairly well, I will definitely need to set aside time to refresh my memory before the exam.
* * *	This is a good book for the exam, but it's been a long time since I read it. I need to review it in detail and probably even reread parts.

<u>Note:</u> If you could not identify at least two works of literature for Question 1 above, be sure to read such works before the exam. If you need help, speak with your teacher.

4-2 Carrying Out The Writing Task

THE PROCESS OF WRITING

Writing is a process made up of several steps. You can use this process to plan and write your response to the Composition prompt.

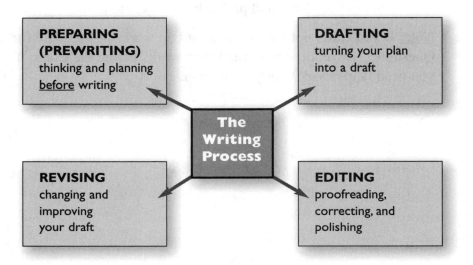

The four basic steps of the writing process are: preparing, drafting, revising, and editing. Let's look at these steps.

- **Preparing:** The first step, often called **prewriting**, is careful thinking and planning. You need to plan both the content and the organization of your essay.
- **Drafting:** Once you have a plan or outline, you're ready to begin writing. You'll probably want to make adjustments to your plan as you go along.
- **Revising:** After putting your ideas down on paper, you'll want to reread and think about what you've written. You can rearrange ideas, add or take out details, change wording, and make other changes to improve your work.
- **Editing:** The last step is proofreading and polishing your paper. You can fix errors in grammar and punctuation, check spelling, fine-tune language, and make any other changes that you think will add to the clarity and quality of your writing.

Making the Process Work for You

You have great flexibility in how you carry out the writing process. You may make a plan, start writing, and then decide to stop and change your plan before continuing. You may finish your first draft and decide that it needs major revision—or just light editing.

The point is that there is no one correct way to use the writing process. You can adjust or expand its steps to meet the demands of the task and your needs as a writer. You can make the process work for you.

TIP: Use Your Time Wisely

How much time should you spend on each step of the writing process? This is a question only you can answer.

Some students find that planning their essay in great detail lets them write their first draft very quickly. Other students feel more comfortable preparing just a brief outline, writing a rough draft, and then spending most of the rest of their time rewriting and revising. As a writer, you need to discover which method works best for you.

However, two rules hold true for everyone: (1) Do at least some basic planning before you begin to write, and (2) always leave enough time to reread your essay from start to finish and make necessary changes and corrections.

Answer in a complete sentence: What are the four steps of the writing process?

_____

_____

_____

_____

Writing for the MCAS Exam

You've probably used the writing process to carry out assignments for school. However, there are some differences when you use the process to respond to the Composition prompt.

First, time is not unlimited. At home, you can spend as many hours as you want planning, writing, and revising a paper. When you take the MCAS exam, you have to compress the writing process into the time available.

Second, when you write a paper at home or in class, you often discuss your work with other students. Maybe you use suggestions from a friend or partner to make revisions. When you write an exam paper, you have to work on your own, using your best judgment.

Despite these differences, however, you can use the four basic steps of the writing process to write a well-developed and well-organized essay for any Composition prompt. In the pages that follow, you'll see how.

Activity C: Understanding the Writing Process

Answer the following questions about the writing process.

1. How can approaching writing as a process help you do your best when you write an essay?

    _____

    _____

    _____

2. Describe how each step of the writing process leads to the next step.

    _____

    _____

    _____

3. Explain the meaning of this statement: "You have great flexibility in how you carry out the writing process."

_____

_____

_____

USING THE WRITING PROCESS

As you read earlier, your essay for the Composition portion of the exam must be tailored to the particular prompt. Let's see how to do this.

Looking Through the Critical Lens

Read the following prompt carefully. Look for key words and phrases. Think about the critical lens statement.

> Literature shows us the human soul, revealing both the bright side of our nature and the dark.
>
> **Assignment:**
>
> Choose a work of literature that you have read in or out of class that illustrates this statement. Write an essay in which you explain how the qualities and actions of the characters suggest the range of human nature.

Once you've thought over the critical lens statement, you have to decide which work of literature to write about. Be sure to choose a book that illustrates the statement and that you can use to carry out the assignment. For this prompt, you need to choose a book in which "the qualities and actions of the characters suggest the range of human nature."

Activity D: Choosing a Work of Literature

1. Write the title and author of a book that you could use to respond to the prompt on page 219.

_____

_____

_____

2. For the book you chose, what "qualities and actions of the characters" would you write about in your essay?

_____

_____

_____

Preparing to Write

You've thought carefully about the critical lens statement. You've decided on a work of literature to write about. Now you're ready to plan the content and organization of your essay. Use the following strategies, always keeping in mind the prompt and the critical lens statement.

- **Determine your controlling idea.** The controlling idea is the principal point that you're making, the main focus of your essay. The controlling idea is also known as the central point or the *thesis*.

In a sense, the controlling idea is like a thread tying together all the paragraphs of your essay. It should relate directly to the prompt and to the work of literature you're writing about.

Usually, you can reword or paraphrase the critical lens or the prompt into a statement of your controlling idea. The sentence that expresses the controlling idea is commonly called the thesis statement. For example, the controlling idea for a response to the prompt on page 219 might be stated this way:

In [title of book], author's name reveals the bright side of human nature as well as the dark side.

or

The qualities and actions of the characters in [title of book] show how good or bad people can be.

Your controlling idea should be clear and specific. If it isn't, you'll have trouble keeping your essay focused.

- **Gather supporting details to develop your ideas.** You will need to develop your controlling idea and the main points of your essay with specific examples and details. Gathering these examples and details is a key part of preparing (prewriting), the first step of the writing process.

You can use various techniques to help you plan your essay. Some of these techniques are described in the box on pages 222-223.

Using Planning (Prewriting) Techniques

- **Brainstorming** is a way to identify ideas and supporting details and examples. When you brainstorm, you list as many ideas, details, and examples as you can think of relating to your topic. Don't worry about which ones are good or bad. Just get your thoughts down on paper. Jot down words, phrases, or whole sentences in whatever order you think of them. When you have a substantial list, look it over. Mark the items that you think would work best in your essay.

- **Mapping**, also called **clustering** or **diagramming**, is a technique that helps you visualize what you're going to write. Using some combination of circles, boxes, lines, and arrows, you create a picture of the ideas and supporting details and examples you plan to include in your essay. Because mapping helps you see relationships between ideas and details, it's useful not only for gathering information but also for planning how to organize it. Here's one example of what a "map" for a three-paragraph essay might look like:

Paragraph 1 (introduction)
Main Idea ——————
Supporting details/examples:
——————————————
——————————————
——————————————

Paragraph 2
Main Idea ——————
Supporting details/examples:
——————————————
——————————————
——————————————

Paragraph 3
Main Idea ——————
Supporting details/examples:
——————————————
——————————————
——————————————

- **Outlining**, like mapping, is useful for both gathering and organizing information. When you write from an outline, you'll often find that each main idea with its supporting details becomes a separate paragraph in your draft. You can take a formal or informal approach to outlining. Compare these examples:

INFORMAL OUTLINE   FORMAL OUTLINE

Idea	**I. Idea**
Supporting detail/example	A. Supporting detail/example
—related detail	1. related detail
—related detail	2. related detail
Supporting detail/example	B. Supporting detail/example
—related detail	1. related detail
—related detail	2. related detail

- **Freewriting** is writing about a topic without stopping for five or ten minutes or longer. Freewriting is similar to brainstorming in that you don't stop to judge which ideas are good or bad as you write them. You just get some thoughts down on paper. When you're finished, you can underline ideas, details, and even whole sentences to use in your essay. Freewriting can help you get started if you can't figure out how to begin—or help you restart if you get stuck.

- **Have a clear plan.** In Part 2, you saw the value of making a plan when you respond to an open-response question. Having a plan is even more important for the Composition portion of the exam, because you're writing a full-length essay.

Your plan may take the form of a formal or informal outline, as shown in the box above. Or you may prefer to structure your plan in some other way, such as a list of key points. Use whatever method helps you organize your ideas, examples, and details most clearly.

Plan on having as many paragraphs as you need to make your points effectively. There is no required number. However, your goal should be to write an essay that is at least three or four paragraphs long.

Don't worry about including more information in your outline than necessary. Instead, when you've finished your outline, review it carefully and cross out any items that are unimportant or irrelevant.

Fill in the blanks: Although there is no required length, your essay should be at least _____ or _____ paragraphs long.

Activity E: Planning an Essay

I. Review the prompt on page 219 and your answers for Activity D on page 220. On a sheet of paper, use the strategies you've learned to help you make a plan for a critical essay responding to the prompt.

2. Exchange papers with a partner. Evaluate each other's plans. Offer your partner specific and constructive suggestions.

<u>Note:</u> Save your plan and the suggestions your partner makes about it for later use in Activity G (page 226).

Looking at a Sample Plan

Let's see how one student planned an essay in response to the prompt on page 219. Later, you'll see how the student used this plan to write an essay. Study the plan on the next page.

Sample Plan

<u>Note:</u> This sample plan may be more detailed or less detailed than yours would be. Your plan should be as detailed as necessary for you to know what you intend to write.

FIRST PARAGRAPH (INTRODUCTION)

  Controlling idea: characters show bright side & dark side of human nature

  Book/author: <u>Of Mice and Men</u> by John Steinbeck

BODY PARAGRAPHS

  Main characters: George & Lennie
      —simple, honest, hardworking
      —basically good people
      —Lennie like a child

  George-Lennie relationship = good aspects of human nature
      -George cares for & protects Lennie
      -friendship, loyalty, trust

  Curley = bad aspects
      —mean troublemaker & bully
      —picks on Lennie
      —wants to kill Lennie at end

  George shoots Lennie to keep from being hunted down or captured
      —Irony: George has to kill Lennie to protect him
      —George's motive for shooting = friendship
      —Curley wanted to shoot him for different
        motive = revenge

LAST PARAGRAPH (CONCLUSION)

  Qualities & actions of George & Lennie vs. Curley show range of human nature

Notice that the student included enough specific information to shape an essay. Making this plan helped the student think through and organize ideas and details. With a clear plan to work from, writing should go smoothly.

Also note the following:

- The student began by writing down the controlling idea.
- The student chose to use a loose outline format. Supporting details and examples are indented under main ideas.
- The student carefully selected ideas and details that relate to the controlling idea.
- The plan does not include all the content that will appear in the actual essay. Instead, the student included just enough ideas and details to create a basic road map of the essay.

Activity F: Evaluating a Plan

Answer the following questions about the student's plan.

1. Overall, what are the strengths of the plan?

_____

_____

_____

2. If this had been your plan, what might you have done differently?

_____

_____

_____

Activity G: Refining Your Plan

1. Review the plan that you made for Activity E on page 224 and the suggestions that you received from your partner. Also compare your plan to the sample student plan on page 225.

2. Make any changes or additions to your plan that you think will help you write your essay.

<u>Note:</u> Save your revised plan for later use in *Activity J* (page 234).

TIP: Use the Same Process for Any Prompt

No matter what kind of prompt you find on the exam, you can use the same basic approach: planning, writing, revising, and editing. For *any* prompt, read the directions carefully and look for key words that explain the writing task. For a prompt that includes a critical lens statement, use the statement to help focus your response. For additional suggestions, review the section *Responding to a Specific Prompt*, pages 213-215.

Writing a First Draft

After you've determined your controlling idea, gathered supporting details, and made a plan, you're ready to write. Here are some guidelines that will help.

- **Give your essay a sound structure.** While no one approach works for every essay, here are a few basics to keep in mind. Remember, though, that these are only guidelines. Don't force a structure onto your writing. That is, don't impose a formula that makes your writing sound artificial.

  Generally, an essay has three parts: an introduction, a body, and a conclusion. The *introduction* introduces the topic and states the controlling idea. The body of the essay consists of the paragraphs that support and develop the controlling idea. The *conclusion* summarizes or reinforces the controlling idea and other main ideas. Sometimes the conclusion is not a separate paragraph, but a sentence or two at the end of your last body paragraph.

  Each paragraph in the body of an essay has its own main idea. You can add structure and clarity to your writing by stating the main idea of a paragraph in a topic sentence. Always develop your main ideas/topic sentences with specific supporting details and examples.

Essay Structure

A typical four-paragraph essay might look like this. Some essays have three paragraphs, while others have five or more. The conclusion is not always a separate paragraph.

Introduction
Controlling idea (thesis statement)

Body Paragraph
Main idea (topic sentence)
Supporting details/examples

Body Paragraph
Main idea (topic sentence)
Supporting details/examples

Conclusion

- **Write a unified essay.** A *unified* essay has a clear controlling idea, and every paragraph in the essay relates to that idea. To write a unified essay, stay focused. Develop and support your controlling idea and omit details that are not related to that idea.

- **Begin with a thesis statement.** State your controlling idea in the first paragraph of your essay. This will help you establish and maintain your focus.
- **Make your style work for you.** Your writing style and choice of language should engage readers and help to communicate your ideas. Follow these tips to do your best writing:

  - Vary sentences in structure and length.
  - Vary your choice of words.
  - Use precise, not vague, language.
  - Don't repeat information unless you want to emphasize it.
  - Use active, not passive, constructions.

- **Organize ideas and details logically.** There are many different ways to organize essay content. Choose an approach that works well for the particular prompt—and one that makes it easy for readers to follow your flow of ideas.

  Three common methods of organization are described below. You can use any of these methods to organize the paragraphs that, together, develop your controlling idea. You can also use these methods to organize information *within* paragraphs—that is, the details and examples that support a paragraph's main idea.

  Note that your essay may not fit neatly into one particular pattern. You may have to combine methods or use different methods in different paragraphs. Or, you may have to take an approach designed specifically for a particular prompt.

  - *Order of increasing importance/interest:* Arrange ideas and supporting details in order from the least important/interesting to the most important/interesting. This form of organization works well when you want to build to a conclusion.

    Order of Increasing Importance/Interest

    third most important idea ➞

    second most important idea ➞

    most important idea of all

  - *Order of decreasing importance/interest:* Arrange ideas and supporting details in order from the most important/interesting to the least important/interesting. This approach works well when you want to lead off with a strong point and then add points.

    Order of Decreasing Importance/Interest

    most important idea ➞

    second most important idea ➞

    third important idea

  - *Chronological order:* Present events or information in time order, usually moving forward in time. You can use this form of organization to describe sequence or explain cause and effect.

Chronological (Time) Order

what happened first ⟶

     what happened next ⟶

          what happened after that

Fill in the blank: Establish the focus of your essay by stating your _____ in the first paragraph.

- **Write coherently.** The word *cohere* comes from Latin and means "stick together." For writing to be coherent, ideas must stick together. In other words, you have to blend them into a smoothly flowing whole.

  You can use *transitional* words and phrases to help make your essay coherent. Study the following chart.

Transitional Words and Phrases

What the Word/Phrase Does	Examples
Gives example	for example, for instance, such as, one reason, in particular
Adds information	also, another, furthermore, in addition, and, besides, too, as well
Indicates a consequence or conclusion	because of, for this reason, therefore, consequently, as a result, finally, lastly
Makes a comparison or signals a change in direction	both, however, on the other hand, but, although, even though, otherwise, on the contrary, in contrast
Adds emphasis	especially, in particular, in fact, above all, most important
Shows sequence	first, second, third (and so on); next; finally; after; before; while; during; later on; then; meanwhile; at last; after a while; immediately

By smoothly connecting ideas and details, transitional words and phrases help readers follow your thinking. Transitional words and phrases often appear at the beginning of a sentence. However, they may also come in the middle or even at the end of a sentence.

Activity H: Using Transitional Words and Phrases

Read the following excerpt from a student's essay and add transitional words or phrases to guide readers smoothly from sentence to sentence. Use the words and phrases shown in the box. Use each one only once.

in fact	**furthermore**	**for instance**
	in contrast	**however**

Atticus Finch in **To Kill a Mockingbird** is an impressive person. He is a man of great bravery and integrity. He is willing to stand up for his beliefs at almost any cost. _____ , Atticus risks
gives example
his life to face a dangerous mob outside the jail.

_____ to Atticus, Bob Ewell has no admirable
makes a comparison
qualities. He is a violent and evil individual. He curses Atticus and spits at him. _____ , it is Ewell who attacks
adds information
Atticus's children.

_____ , Ewell is not the only character in the book
signals change in direction
with negative traits. _____ , most of the town's
adds emphasis
citizens are guilty of prejudice and racism. It is no wonder that Tom Robinson is unfairly charged with rape because of the color of his skin.

Looking at a Sample Essay

Let's see how the student turned the sample plan that you saw earlier into an essay. First, review the prompt on page 219 and the sample plan on page 225.

Now read the student's essay based on the plan. Think about these questions as you read:

- How closely did the student follow the plan's content and organization?
- How well does the essay respond to the prompt?

Sample Essay

1   In his novel Of <u>Mice and Men,</u> John Steinbeck reveals both the bright side of human nature and the dark side. The qualities and actions of the characters show how good or bad people can be.

2   The main characters of the novel are George Milton and Lennie Small. Like several other characters in the book, they are simple, honest men. They work hard and dream of owning their own place. They are basically good people who want no trouble. However, because Lennie is more like an overgrown child than an adult, he can't help but get into trouble.

3   The relationship between George and Lennie shows many positive qualities of human nature. For example, George takes care of his childlike friend and tries to keep him out of trouble. The friendship, loyalty, and trust between these two men is very touching.

4   If George and Lennie represent the bright side of human nature, Curley represents the dark side. Curley is the son of the boss at the ranch. He's a mean troublemaker, who bullies people. He picks on Lennie. At the end, Curley wants to shoot Lennie down after Lennie accidentally kills Curley's wife.

5   Ironically, George shoots his friend to protect him. He wants to save him from being hunted down by Curley or captured and locked up, an even worse fate. George shoots Lennie out of friendship. Curley wanted to shoot him for revenge. This contrast in motives suggests how very different people can be.

6   The characters in <u>Of Mice and Men</u> reveal a great deal about human nature. In many ways, George and Lennie show human nature at its best. Curley, on the other hand, suggests people's darker, unpleasant side.

Read the student's essay a second time and note the following:

- The student has written a well-organized essay, closely following the plan. Of course, the essay is much more filled out than the plan was.
- Paragraph 1 states the controlling idea of the essay.
- Paragraph 1 also names the book and author to be discussed. *When writing about a work of literature, always identify the work in your first paragraph.*
- The essay consists of six paragraphs, including a brief introduction. The last paragraph concludes the essay by summarizing and reinforcing the controlling idea.
- The student develops the controlling idea in paragraphs 2-5, using specific details and examples.
- The student presents ideas and details clearly. These ideas and details respond directly to the prompt assignment: "explain how the qualities and actions of the characters suggest the range of human nature."

Activity I: Examining an Essay

Answer the following questions about the student's essay.

1. Has the student written a unified essay? Explain.

_____

_____

_____

2. How might the student have organized this essay into a different number of paragraphs? Be specific.

_____

_____

_____

3. Paragraph 4 begins with a topic sentence. What is the main idea that the sentence states? How does the rest of the paragraph develop the idea?

_____

_____

_____

4. Give two examples of transitional words or phrases in the essay. Explain what function each word or phrase serves.

_____

_____

_____

5. Give two examples of how the student varied sentences in structure and length.

_____

_____

_____

Activity J: Turning Your Plan into an Essay

Use what you've learned in this chapter to write a first draft based on your revised plan (Activity G, page 226).

Note: Save your draft for later use in Activity L (page 236).

Revising a Draft

After you've finished your first draft, carefully review your work. Your goal is to evaluate your essay and try to improve it. Do this by making any necessary changes in content, organization, paragraph development, language, and other elements of writing.

Don't worry too much about grammar, punctuation, and spelling at this point. After you revise your draft, you can proofread and edit it.

To guide your revision, ask yourself the key questions shown below.

Checklist for Revising Your Essay

✓ Have I fully and specifically answered the prompt?

✓ Have I presented my ideas clearly?

✓ Have I developed my ideas with enough supporting details and examples?

✓ Have I organized my essay in a logical way?

✓ Do my ideas flow smoothly within paragraphs and from one paragraph to the next?

✓ Is my essay clearly focused throughout?

✓ Have I shown variety in sentence structure and word choice?

✓ Are there any places where I can improve my writing style or use of language?

Activity K: Evaluating an Essay

Work with a partner. Review the student's essay on page 232. Then tell whether you agree or disagree with each of the following statements, and *why*. Give specific reasons or examples to support your answers.

1. The student answers the prompt fully and specifically.

_____

_____

_____

2. Ideas flow smoothly within paragraphs and from one paragraph to the next.

_____

_____

_____

3. The essay stays clearly focused throughout.

_____

_____

_____

4. The writing style and use of language help to convey the student's ideas.

_____

_____

_____

Activity L: Revising Your Essay

Use the *Checklist for Revising Your Essay* on page 235 to help you revise the first draft you wrote for *Activity J* on page 234.
<u>Note</u>: Save your revised draft for later use in *Activity M* (page 237).

Editing the Essay

The last step in the writing process is editing and proofreading. Even though you probably did some editing as you were revising your essay, now it's time to focus your attention specifically on fixing errors in grammar and punctuation, checking spelling, and fine-tuning language. In other words, you're polishing and putting the finishing touches on your essay.

To help with your editing, use the following checklist as a starting point.

Checklist for Editing Your Essay

Punctuation and Capitalization

✓ Have I used commas, apostrophes, quotation marks, and periods where needed?
✓ Have I capitalized the first word of every sentence?
✓ Have I capitalized all proper nouns?

Grammar

✓ Have I written complete sentences?
✓ Have I avoided run-on sentences?
✓ Do my subjects and verbs agree?

Spelling

✓ Have I spelled words correctly?
✓ Have I used the words that I meant to use (for example, its/it's, your/you're, there/their, to/too, affect/effect)?

Activity M: Editing Your Essay

Use the *Checklist for Editing Your Essay* above to help you edit the draft you revised for Activity L on page 236.

TIP: Write Neatly

Even the best essay won't receive a high grade if readers can't read it. Always write neatly and legibly. Messy handwriting can lower your score because readers will find it hard to follow your ideas. You can also make reading easier by leaving adequate left and right margins and by indenting the first line of each paragraph.

REVIEW

Here is a brief summary of some of the key strategies you've learned in Part 4. To review any of these in more detail, turn back to the pages indicated.

Responding to any Composition prompt (pages 210-212):

- Read the prompt carefully.
- Look for key words and phrases.

Responding to a prompt with a reading passage (page 213):

- Read the passage at least twice.
- Think about elements and techniques.
- Jot down notes.

Responding to a prompt with a critical lens statement (page 214):

- Consider ahead of time which works of literature you might write about.
- Be ready to write about more than one book.
- Choose substantial works.

Preparing to write (pages 220-227):

- Determine your controlling idea.
- Gather supporting details to develop your ideas.
- Have a clear plan.

Writing a first draft (pages 227-234):

- Give your essay a sound structure.
- Write a unified essay.
- Begin with a thesis statement.
- Make your style work for you.
- Organize ideas and details logically.
- Write coherently.

Revising a draft (pages 235-236):

- Review the *Checklist for Revising Your Essay* on page 235.

Editing the essay (pages 236-237):

- Review the *Checklist for Editing Your Essay* on page 237.

PRACTICE

Use the activities that follow to practice what you learned in Part 4.

Responding to a Prompt with a Critical Lens Statement

Write an essay responding to the following prompt. (You saw this prompt earlier, on page 212.)

> In literature, as in life, people pursue love, truth, happiness, or power. Sometimes they succeed in their quest, sometimes not.
>
> **Assignment:**
> Identify a work of literature that you have read in or out of class that illustrates this statement. Write an essay in which you describe a character's pursuit of "love, truth, happiness, or power." Explain whether or not the character succeeded in his or her quest, and why.

Evaluating an Essay

Exchange papers with a partner. Evaluate your partner's essay on the basis of the following elements. Make your comments as constructive and specific as you can. Your goal is to help your partner improve his or her skills.

Development of ideas:

_____

_____

_____

Organization:

_____

_____

Supporting details:

_____

_____

_____

Language/style:

_____

_____

_____

Sentence structure:

_____

_____

_____

Grammar and word usage:

_____

_____

_____

Spelling, capitalization, punctuation:

_____

_____

_____

Improving and Polishing Your Essay

Use your partner's comments to help you further revise and polish your essay. Make whatever changes you think will improve your work.

Responding to a Prompt with a Reading Passage

Write an essay responding to the following prompt. (You saw this prompt earlier, on page 211)

Read the following opening paragraphs from a short story by Jack London. When you have finished reading, respond to the writing assignment that follows.

To Build a Fire
By Jack London

For land travel or seafaring, the world over, a companion is usually considered desirable. In the Klondike, as Tom Vincent found out, such a companion is absolutely essential. But he found it out, not by precept, but through bitter experience.

"Never travel alone," is a precept of the north. He had heard it many times and laughed; for he was a strapping young fellow, big-boned and big-muscled, with faith in himself and in the strength of his head and hands.

It was on a bleak January day when the experience came that taught him respect for the frost, and for the wisdom of the men who had battled with it.

He had left Calumet Camp on the Yukon with a light pack on his back, to go up Paul Creek to the divide between it and Cherry Creek, where his party was prospecting and hunting moose.

The frost was sixty degree below zero, and he had thirty miles of lonely trail to cover, but he did not mind. In fact, he enjoyed it, swinging along through the silence, his blood pounding warmly through his veins, and his mind carefree and happy. For he and his comrades were certain they had struck "pay" up there on the Cherry Creek Divide; and, further, he was returning to them from Dawson with cheery home letters from the States.

Assignment:

In many literary works, the opening paragraphs offer clues to events that follow. Read the above paragraphs for such clues. Based on these clues, write an essay discussing what might happen in this story. In developing your essay, think about the significance of the first paragraph and consider such elements of the passage as word choice, point of view, tone, mood, setting, and characters.

Evaluating an Essay

Exchange papers with a partner. Evaluate your partner's essay on the basis of the following elements. Make your comments as constructive and specific as you can. Your goal is to help your partner improve his or her skills.

Development of ideas:

_____

_____

_____

Organization:

_____

_____

_____

Supporting details:

_____

_____

_____

_____

Language/style:

_____

_____

_____

Sentence structure:

_____

_____

_____

Grammar and word usage:

_____

_____

_____

Spelling, capitalization, punctuation:

_____

_____

_____

Improving and Polishing Your Essay

Use your partner's comments to help you further revise and polish your essay. Make whatever changes you think will improve your work.

PRACTICE TEST

LANGUAGE AND LITERATURE

The following excerpt is from the opening pages of Rachel Carson's book Silent Spring. At the time the book was published, 1962, farmers routinely used pesticides without considering their effects. Carson's book changed the way people thought about chemicals in the environment. Read the excerpt carefully. Then answer the questions that follow.

A Fable for Tomorrow
by Rachel Carson

1   There was once a town in the heart of America where all life seemed to live in harmony with its surroundings. The town lay in the midst of a checkerboard of prosperous farms, with fields of grain and hillsides of orchards where, in spring, white clouds of bloom drifted above the green fields. In autumn, oak and maple and birch set up a blaze of color that flamed and flickered across a backdrop of pines. Then foxes barked in the hills and deer silently crossed the fields, half hidden in the mists of the fall mornings.

2   Along the roads, laurel, viburnum and alder, great ferns and wildflowers delighted the traveler's eye through much of the year. Even in winter the roadsides were places of beauty where countless birds came to feed on the berries and on the seed heads of the dried weeds rising above the snow. The countryside was, in fact, famous for the abundance and variety of its bird life, and when the flood of migrants was pouring through in spring and fall people traveled from great distances to observe them. Others came to fish the streams, which flowed clear and cold out of the hills and contained shady pools where trout lay. So it had been from the days many years ago when the first settlers raised their houses, sank their wells, and built their barns.

3   Then a strange blight crept over the area and everything began to change. Some evil spell had settled on the community: mysterious maladies swept the flocks of chickens; the cattle and sheep sickened and died. Everywhere was a shadow of death. The farmers spoke of much illness among their families. In the town the doctors had become more and more puzzled by new kinds of sickness appearing among their patients. There had been several sudden and unexplained deaths, not only among adults but even among children, who would be stricken suddenly while at play and die within a few hours.

There was a strange stillness. The birds, for example—where had they gone? Many people spoke of them, puzzled and disturbed. The feeding stations in the backyards were deserted. The few birds seen anywhere were moribund; they trembled violently and could not fly. It was a spring

4   without voices. On the mornings that had once throbbed with the dawn chorus of robins, catbirds, doves, jays, wrens, and scores of other bird voices there was now no sound; only silence lay over the fields and woods and marsh.

On the farms the hens brooded, but no chicks hatched. The farmers complained that they were unable to raise any pigs—the litters were small
5   and the young survived only a few days. The apple trees were coming into bloom but no bees droned among the blossoms, so there was no pollination and there would be no fruit.

The roadsides, once so attractive, were now lined with browned and withered vegetation as though swept by fire. These, too, were silent,
6   deserted by all living things. Even the streams were now lifeless. Anglers no longer visited them, for all the fish had died.

In the gutters under the eaves and between the shingles of the roofs, a
7   white granular powder still showed a few patches; some weeks before it had fallen like snow upon the roofs and the lawns, the fields and streams.

No witchcraft, no enemy action had silenced the rebirth of new life in
8   this stricken world. The people had done it themselves.

This town does not actually exist, but it might easily have a thousand counterparts in America or elsewhere in the world. I know of no community that has experienced all the misfortunes I described. Yet every one of these disasters has actually happened somewhere, and many real communities have already suffered a substantial number of them. A grim specter has crept upon us almost unnoticed, and this imagined tragedy may easily become a stark reality we all shall know.

Multiple-Choice Questions

1. The author's purpose for writing is to

   A. warn people of a danger.

   B. tell an entertaining story.

   C. persuade people to move elsewhere.

   D. encourage people to become farmers.

2. How does the author make her point?

   A. by telling in detail what happened to her home town

   B. by presenting arguments against the use of chemicals

   C. by describing a tragic historical event

   D. by comparing a town before and after pesticide use

3. In paragraph 4, what does the word *moribund* mean?

   A. colorful

   B. hungry

   C. dying

   D. noisy

4. The author writes, "The roadsides, once so attractive, were now lined with browned and withered vegetation as though swept by fire." This is an example of

   A. satire.

   B. simile.

   C. metaphor.

   D. personification.

5. Which is **not** described in the excerpt as an effect on the town?

   A. People and animals became sick.

   B. Trees did not bear fruit.

   C. Children had to stay at home.

   D. All the fish died.

Open-Response Question

6. Using information from the excerpt, explain why Carson views pesticides as destructive.

_____

_____

_____

_____

_____

_____

The following selection is an excerpt from the short story "Dead Men's Path" by Nigerian writer Chinua Achebe. The main character, Mr. Michael Obi, has been appointed the new headmaster of Ndume Central School. Mr. Obi has definite ideas about how a school should be run. Read the excerpt carefully. Then answer the questions that follow.

Dead Men's Path
by Chinua Achebe

1 Ndume School was backward in every sense of the word. Mr. Obi put his whole life into the work, and his wife hers too. He had two aims. A high standard of teaching was insisted upon, and the school compound was to be turned into a place of beauty. Nancy's dream-gardens came to life with the coming of the rains, and blossomed. Beautiful hibiscus and allamanda hedges in brilliant red and yellow marked out the carefully tended school compound from the rank neighborhood bushes.

2 One evening as Obi was admiring his work he was scandalized to see an old woman from the village hobble right across the compound, through a marigold flower-bed and the hedges. On going up there he found faint signs of an almost disused path from the village across the school compound to the bush on the other side.

3 "It amazes me," said Obi to one of his teachers who had been three years in the school, "that you people allowed the villagers to make use of this footpath. It is simply incredible." He shook his head.

4 "The path," said the teacher apologetically, "appears to be very important to them. Although it is hardly used, it connects the village shrine with their place of burial."

5 "And what has that got to do with the school?" asked the headmaster.

"Well, I don't know," replied the other with a shrug of the shoulders.

6 "But I remember there was a big row some time ago when we attempted to close it."

7 "That was some time ago. But it will not be used now," said Obi as he walked away. "What will the Government Education Officer think of this when he comes to inspect the schoolroom next week? The villagers might, for all I know, decide to use the schoolroom for a pagan ritual during the inspection."

8 Heavy sticks were planted closely across the path at the two places where it entered and left the school premises. These were further strengthened with barbed wire.

9 Three days later the village priest of *Ani* called on the headmaster. He was an old man and walked with a slight stoop. He carried a stout walking-stick which he usually tapped on the floor, by way of emphasis, each time he made a new point in his argument.

10   "I have heard," he said after the usual exchange of cordialities, "that our ancestral footpath has recently been closed . . ."

11   "Yes," replied Mr. Obi. "We cannot allow people to make a highway of our school compound."

12   "Look here, my son," said the priest bringing down his walking-stick, "this path was here before you were born and before your father was born. The whole life of this village depends on it. Our dead relatives depart by it and our ancestors visit us by it. But most important, it is the path of children coming in to be born . . ."

13   Mr. Obi listened with a satisfied smile on his face.

14   "The whole purpose of our school," he said finally, "is to eradicate just such beliefs as that. Dead men do not require footpaths. The whole idea is just fantastic. Our duty is to teach your children to laugh at such ideas."

15   "What you say may be true," replied the priest, "but we follow the practices of our fathers. If you re-open the path we shall have nothing to quarrel about. What I always say is: let the hawk perch and let the eagle perch." He rose to go.

16   "I am sorry," said the young headmaster. "But the school compound cannot be a thoroughfare. It is against our regulations. I would suggest your constructing another path, skirting our premises. We can even get our boys to help in building it. I don't suppose the ancestors will find the little detour too burdensome."

17   "I have no more words to say," said the old priest, already outside.

18   Two days later a young woman in the village died in childbed. A diviner was immediately consulted and he prescribed heavy sacrifices to propitiate ancestors insulted by the fence.

19   Obi woke up next morning among the ruins of his work. The beautiful hedges were torn up not just near the path but right round the school, the flowers trampled to death and one of the school buildings pulled down . . . That day, the white Supervisor came to inspect the school and wrote a nasty report on the state of the premises but more seriously about the "tribal-war situation developing between the school and the village, arising in part from the misguided zeal of the new headmaster."

Multiple-Choice Questions

7. This excerpt is an example of

   A. persuasive writing.

   B. narrative writing.

   C. technical writing.

   D. informative writing.

8. Which word is closest to the meaning of *scandalized* in paragraph 2?

   A. frightened

   B. delighted

   C. shocked

   D. amused

9. Heavy sticks were planted in two places along the footpath in order to

   A. guide villagers safely across the school grounds.

   B. block villagers from crossing the school grounds.

   C. fence in the village shrine.

   D. keep out the villagers' ancestors.

10. How did Mr. Obi feel about the villagers' beliefs?

    A. He respected them.

    B. He held them in contempt.

    C. He found them harmless and amusing.

    D. He thought they endangered the teachers.

11. When a young woman of the village died giving birth, the villagers

    A. blamed the fence.

    B. thought that Mr. Obi had killed her.

    C. complained to the Supervisor who came to inspect the school.

    D. held the priest responsible.

12. Based on events in the story, what word do you think the author would use to describe Mr. Obi?

     A. considerate

     B. uncertain

     C. impressive

     D. arrogant

Open-Response Question

13. There is a biblical saying that "pride goeth before destruction, and an haughty spirit before a fall." How does that saying apply to this story? Support your answer with details from the excerpt.

_____

_____

_____

_____

_____

_____

In 1963, civil rights leader Martin Luther King, Jr. , gave his most famous speech before a crowd of 250,000 people on the steps of the Lincoln Memorial in Washington, D.C. The following selection is an excerpt from that speech. Read the excerpt carefully and then answer the questions that follow.

I Have a Dream

by Martin Luther King, Jr.

1 We've come here today to dramatize a shameful condition. In a sense we've come to our nation's capital to cash a check. When the architects of our republic wrote the magnificent words of the Constitution and the Declaration of Independence, they were signing a promissory note[1] to which every American was to fall heir. This note was the promise that all men, yes, black men as well as white men, would be guaranteed the unalienable right of life, liberty, and the pursuit of happiness.

2 It is obvious today that America has defaulted on[2] this promissory note in so far as her citizens of color are concerned. Instead of honoring this sacred obligation, America has given the Negro people a bad check; a check which has come back marked "insufficient funds." We refuse to believe that there are insufficient funds in the great vaults of opportunity of this nation. And so we've come to cash this check that will give us upon demand the riches of freedom and the security of justice.

3 We have also come to this hallowed spot to remind America of the fierce urgency of now. This is no time to engage in the luxury of cooling off or to take the tranquilizing drug of gradualism. *Now* is the time to make real the promises of democracy; *now* is the time to rise from the dark and desolate valley of segregation to the sunlit path of racial justice; *now* is the time to lift our nation from the quicksands of racial injustice to the solid rock of brotherhood; *now* is the time to make justice a reality for all God's children. It would be fatal for the nation to overlook the urgency of the moment. This sweltering summer of the Negro's legitimate discontent will not pass until there is an invigorating autumn of freedom and equality.

[1] A written promise to pay money; an IOU.

[2] Failed to keep (the promise).

Multiple-Choice Questions

14. In paragraph 2, King says that "America has defaulted on this promissory note . . . " This is an example of

    A. allegory.

    B. alliteration.

    C. oxymoron.

    D. metaphor.

15. King emphasizes the main idea of paragraph 3 by

    A. repeating the phrase "**now** is the time to . . . " several times.

    B. talking about the importance of democracy.

    C. using the phrase "racial injustice."

    D. mentioning the Constitution.

16. What is the "shameful condition" to which King refers in paragraph 1?

    A. America does not have enough money to cash people's checks.

    B. The democratic system no longer works.

    C. America has failed to provide equal opportunities to all people.

    D. America's people no longer have the rights guaranteed by the Declaration of Independence.

1de·fault \di-ʹfȯlt, dē; ʹdē-,fȯlt\ *n* [ME *defaute, defaulte,* fr. OF *defaute,* fr. *defaillir* to be lacking, fail, fr. *de-* + *faillir* to fail] (13c) **1:** failure to do something required by duty or law': NEGLECT **2:** *archaic:* FAULT **3:** a failure to pay financial debts **4 a:** failure to appear at the required time in a legal proceeding **b:** a failure to compete in or to finish an appointed contest **5:** a selection automatically used by a computer program in the absence of a choice made by the user—**in default of** : in the absence of

---

17. According to the dictionary entry above, the word *default* originated in which language?

    A. Middle English

    B. French

    C. Greek

    D. Latin

Open-Response Question

18. Imagery makes King's speech come alive. Choose two images
    that King uses and explain what effect each image creates.

_____

_____

_____

_____

_____

_____

In this short play, Betty Keller examines the life of two elderly sisters. As you read, think about the characters and their situation. When you have finished reading, answer the questions that follow.

Tea Party

by Betty Keller

CHARACTERS

Alma Evans: *seventy-five years old, small and spare framed. Her clothing is simple but not outdated, her grey hair cut short and neat. She walks with the aid of a cane.*

Hester Evans: *seventy-nine years old. There is little to distinguish her physically from her sister, except perhaps a face a little more pinched and pain-worn. She sits in a wheelchair.*

The Boy: *in his early teens, seen only fleetingly.*

SCENE. *The sitting room of the Evans sisters' home. The door to the street is on the rear wall. Upstage Left, (a large window face the street Upstage Center. On the right wall is the door to the kitchen; on the left, a door to the remainder of the house. Downstage Left is an easy chair. Upstage Right a sofa, Downstage Right a tea trolley. The room is crowded with the knicknacks gathered by its inhabitants in three-quarters of a century of living.*

[At rise, ALMA is positioning HESTER'S wheelchair Upstage Left. ALMA'S cane is on HESTER'S lap.]

1   HESTER.   That's it.
[ALMA takes her cane from HESTER. They both survey the room.]
ALMA.   I think I'll sit on the sofa . . . at the far end.
HESTER.   Yes. That will be cozy. Then he can sit on this end between us.
[ALMA sits on the Downstage Right end of the sofa. They both study the effect.]
ALMA.   But then he's too close to the door, Hester!
[HESTER nods, absorbed in the problem.]
2   ALMA.   *[Moving to the Upstage Left end of sofa.]*
Then I'd better sit here.
HESTER.   But now he's too far away from me, Alma.
[ALMA stands; both of them study the room again.]
ALMA.   But if I push the tea trolley in front of you, he'll have to come to you, won't he?
HESTER.   Oh, all right, Alma. You're sure it's today?
[ALMA. Pushing the tea trolley laden with cups and napkins, etc. to HESTER.]

	ALMA	The first Thursday of the month.
10	HESTER.	You haven't forgotten the chocolate biscuits?
	ALMA.	No dear, they're on the plate. I'll bring them in with the tea. [*Goes to the window, peering up the street to the Right.*]
	HESTER.	And cocoa?
	ALMA.	I remembered.
	HESTER.	You didn't remember for Charlie's visit.
15	ALMA.	Charlie drinks tea, Hester. I didn't make cocoa for him because he drinks tea.
	HESTER.	Oh. He didn't stay last time anyway.
	ALMA.	It was a busy day . . .
	HESTER.	Rushing in and out like that. I was going to tell him about father and the *Bainbridge* . . . and he didn't stay.
	ALMA.	What about the *Bainbridge*?
20	HESTER.	Her maiden voyage out of Liverpool . . . when father was gone three months and we thought he'd gone down with her.
	ALMA.	That wasn't the *Bainbridge*.
	HESTER.	Yes, it was. It was the *Bainbridge*. I remember standing on the dock in the snow when she finally came in. That was the year I'd begun first form, and I could spell out the letters on her side.
	ALMA.	It was her sister ship, the *Heddingham*.
	HESTER.	The *Bainbridge*. You were too young to remember. Let's see, the year was . . .
25	ALMA.	Mother often told the story. It was the *Heddingham* and her engine broke down off Cape Wrath beyond the Hebrides.
	HESTER.	It was 1902 and you were just four years old.
	ALMA.	The *Heddingham,* and she limped into port on January the fifth.
	HESTER.	January the fourth just after nine in the morning, and we stood in the snow and watched the *Bainbridge* nudge the pier, and I cried and the tears froze on my cheeks.
	ALMA.	The *Heddingham*.
30	HESTER.	Alma, mother didn't cry, you know. I don't think she ever cried. My memory of names and places is sharp so that I don't confuse them as some others I could mention, but sometimes I can't remember things like how people reacted. But I remember that day. There were tears frozen on my cheeks but mother didn't cry.
	ALMA.	[*Nodding.*] She said he didn't offer a word of explanation. Just marched home beside her.
	HESTER.	[*smiling.*] He never did say much . . . Is he coming yet?
	ALMA.	No, can't be much longer though. Almost half past four.
	HESTER.	Perhaps you'd better bring in the tea. Then it will seem natural.
35	ALMA.	Yes dear, I know. [*Exits out door Upstage Right.*] Everything's ready.
	HESTER.	What will you talk about?

ALMA.   [*Re-entering with the teapot*] I thought perhaps . . . [*Carefully putting down the teapot.*] . . . perhaps brother George!

HESTER.   And the torpedo? No, Alma, he's not old enough for that story!

ALMA.   He's old enough to know about courage. I thought I'd show him the medal, too. [*She goes to the window, peers both ways worriedly, then carries on towards the kitchen.*]

40   HESTER.   Not yet? He's late tonight. You're sure it's today?

ALMA.   He'll come. It's the first Thursday. [*Exit.*]

HESTER.   You have his money?

ALMA.   [*Returning with the plate of biscuits.*] I've got a twenty-dollar bill, Hester.

HESTER.   Alma!

45   ALMA.   Well, we haven't used that one on him. It was Dennis, the last one, who always had change. We could get two visits this way, Hester.

HESTER.   Maybe Dennis warned him to carry change for a twenty.

ALMA.   It seemed worth a try. [*Goes to the window again.*] Are you going to tell him about the *Heddingham*?

HESTER.   The *Bainbridge.* Maybe . . . or maybe I'll tell him about the day the Great War ended. Remember, Alma, all the noise, the paper streamers . .

ALMA.   And father sitting silent in his chair.

50   HESTER.   It wasn't the same for him with George gone. Is he coming yet?

ALMA.   No dear, maybe he's stopped to talk somewhere. [*Looking to the right*] . . . No, . . . no, there he is, on the Davis' porch now!

HESTER.   I'll pour then. You get the cocoa, Alma.

ALMA.   [*Going out.*] It's all ready, I just have to add hot water.

HESTER.   Don't forget the marshmallows!

55   ALMA.   [*Reappearing*] Oh, Hester, what if he comes in and just sits down closest to the door? He'll never stay!

HESTER.   You'll have to prod him along. For goodness sakes, Alma, get his cocoa!
[*ALMA disappears*]

HESTER.   He must be nearly here. He doesn't go to the Leschynskis, and the Blackburns don't get home till after six.

ALMA.   [*Returning with the cocoa.*] Here we are! Just in . . . [*The* BOY *passes the window. There is a slapping sound as the newspaper lands on the porch.*]

[*ALMA and HESTER look at the door and wait, hoping to hear a knock, but they both know the truth. Finally, ALMA goes to the door, opens it and looks down at the newspaper.*]

ALMA.   He's gone on by.

60   HESTER.   You must have had the day wrong.

ALMA.   No, he collected at the Davis'.

HESTER.   [*After a long pause.*] He couldn't have forgotten us.

ALMA.   [*Still holding the cocoa, she turns from the door.*] He's collecting at the Kerighan's now. [*She closes the door and stands forlornly.*]

HESTER.   Well, don't stand there with that cocoa! You look silly. [ALMA *brings the cocoa to the tea trolley.*] Here's your tea. [ALMA *takes the cup, sits on the Upstage Left end of the sofa. There is a long silence.*]

65   HESTER.   I think I'll save that story for the meter man.

ALMA.   The *Heddingham*?

HESTER.   The *Bainbridge.*

ALMA.   [*After a pause.*] They don't read the meters for two more weeks.

Multiple-Choice Questions

19. As the play begins, Alma and Hester are preparing for the arrival of

    A. brother George.

    B. their father.

    C. a neighbor.

    D. the paperboy.

20. Referring to the twenty-dollar bill, Alma tells her sister that "we haven't used that one on him" (line 44). What does she mean?

    A. She usually pays the boy with a ten-dollar bill.

    B. The twenty-dollar bill will require the boy to return with change.

    C. The sisters are fond of playing practical jokes.

    D. She plans to give the boy an especially large tip.

21. The sisters can best be described as

    A. lonely.

    B. suspicious.

    C. mean.

    D. menacing.

22. Events in the play suggest that

    A. a tea party is an enjoyable way to meet people.

    B. teenage boys cannot be trusted.

    C. the lives of elderly people can be very empty.

    D. people in their seventies are unable to care for themselves.

Open-Response Question

23. Based on the play, how would you describe the daily lives of
    Alma and Hester? Use specific details from the play to support
    your answer.

_____

_____

_____

_____

_____

_____

When she was less than two years old, a serious illness left Helen Keller blind and deaf. Her teacher and friend Anne Sullivan taught her sign language, and eventually Helen Keller became a world-famous writer and lecturer. In the following excerpt, Keller describes her first experiences with Anne Sullivan. Read the excerpt carefully. Then answer the questions that follow.

The Story of My Life
by Helen Keller

1 The most important day I remember in all my life is the one on which my teacher, Anne Mansfield Sullivan, came to me. I am filled with wonder when I consider the immeasurable contrasts between the two lives which it connects. It was the third of March, 1887, three months before I was seven years old.

2 On the afternoon of that eventful day, I stood on the porch, wondering, expectant. I guessed vaguely from my mother's signs and from the hurrying to and fro in the house that something unusual was about to happen, so I went to the door and waited on the steps. The afternoon sun penetrated the mass of honeysuckle that covered the porch, and fell on my upturned face. My fingers lingered almost unconsciously on the familiar leaves and blossoms which had just come forth to greet the sweet southern spring. I did not know what the future held of marvel or surprise for me.

3 Have you ever been at sea in a dense fog, when it seemed as if darkness shut you in, and the great ship, tense and anxious, groped her way toward the shore and you waited with beating heart for something to happen? I was like that ship before my education began, only I was without compass or sounding-line, and had no way of knowing how near the harbor was. "Light! Give me light!" was the wordless cry of my soul, and the light of love shone on me in that very hour.

4 I felt approaching footsteps. I stretched out my hand as I supposed to my mother. Someone took it, and I was caught up and held close in the arms of her who had come to reveal all things to me, and, more than all things else, to love me.

5 The morning after my teacher came she led me into her room and gave me a doll. When I had played with it a little while, Miss Sullivan slowly spelled into my hand the word "d-o-l-l." I was at once interested in this finger play and tried to imitate it. When I finally succeeded in making the letters correctly I was flushed with childish pleasure and pride. Running downstairs to my mother I held up my hand and made the letters for doll. I did not know that I was spelling a word or even that words existed; I was simply making my fingers go in monkey-like imitation. In the days that followed I learned to spell in this uncomprehending way a great many words, among them *pin, hat, cup* and a few verbs like *sit, stand* and *walk*. But my teacher had been with me several weeks before I understood that everything has a name.

One day, while I was playing with my new doll, Miss Sullivan put my big doll into my lap also, spelled "d-o-l-l" and tried to make me understand that "d-o-l-l applied to both. Earlier in the day we had had a tussle over the words "m-u-g" and "w-a-t-e-r." Miss Sullivan had tried to impress it upon me that "m-u-g" is *mug* and "w-a-t-e-r" is *water,* but I persisted in confounding the two. In despair she had dropped the subject for the time, only to renew it at the first opportunity. I became impatient at her repeated attempts and, seizing the new doll, I dashed it upon the floor. I was keenly

6 delighted when I felt the fragments of the broken doll at my feet. Neither sorrow nor regret followed my passionate outburst. I had not loved the doll. In the still, dark world in which I lived there was no strong sentiment or tenderness. I felt my teacher sweep the fragments to one side of the hearth, and I had a sense of satisfaction that the cause of my discomfort was removed. She brought me my hat, and I knew I was going out into the warm sunshine. This thought, if a wordless sensation may be called a thought, made me hop and skip with pleasure.

We walked down the path to the well-house, attracted by the fragrance of the honeysuckle with which it was covered. Someone was drawing water and my teacher placed my hand under the spout. As the cool stream gushed over one hand she spelled into the other the word *water,* first slowly, then rapidly. I stood still, my whole attention fixed upon the motions of her fingers. Suddenly I felt a misty consciousness as of

7 something forgotten—a thrill of returning thought; and somehow the mystery of language was revealed to me. I knew then that "w-a-t-e-r" meant the wonderful cool something that was flowing over my hand. The living word awakened my soul, gave it light, hope, joy, set it free! There were barriers still, it is true, but barriers that could in time be swept away.

I left the well-house eager to learn. Everything had a name, and each name gave birth to a new thought. As we returned to the house every object which I touched seemed to quiver with life. That was because I saw everything with the strange, new sight that had come to me. On entering

8 the door I remembered the doll I had broken. I felt my way to the hearth and picked up the pieces. I tried vainly to put them together. Then my eyes filled with tears; for I realized what I had done, and for the first time I felt repentance and sorrow.

I learned a great many new words that day. I do not remember what they all were; but I do know that *mother, father, sister, teacher* were

9 among them—words that were to make the world blossom for me. It would have been difficult to find a happier child than I was as I lay in my crib at the close of that eventful day and lived over the joys it had brought me, and for the first time longed for a new day to come.

Multiple-Choice Questions

24. This excerpt is an example of

    A. autobiography.

    B. hyperbole.

    C. symbolism.

    D. biography.

25. To express her meaning in paragraph 3, Keller uses

    A. personification.

    B. irony.

    C. figurative language.

    D. onomatopoeia.

26. Which event in this excerpt was most significant for Helen Keller?

    A. She touched the honeysuckle leaves and blossoms.

    B. She smashed her new doll.

    C. She discovered that words referred to objects.

    D. She learned to spell doll with her fingers.

27. In paragraph 8, what does the word *repentance* mean?

    A. regret

    B. anger

    C. awe

    D. pride

28. What is the tone at the end of the excerpt?

    A. annoyed

    B. fearful

    C. uncertain

    D. optimistic

29. In the third sentence of paragraph 8, "to quiver" is an example of

   A. a present participle.

   B. a past participle.

   C. an infinitive.

   D. an object of a preposition.

Open-Response Question

30. Explain how Anne Sullivan dramatically changed Helen Keller's life. Use information from the excerpt to support your answer.

_____

_____

_____

_____

_____

_____

Read the poem "Shoulders." As you read, think about how the poet uses a symbolic image to convey the poem's meaning. Then answer the questions that follow.

Shoulders

by Naomi Shihab Nye

1   A man crosses the street in rain,
    stepping gently, looking two times north and south,
    because his son is asleep on his shoulder.

    No car must splash him.
5   No car drive too near to his shadow.

    This man carries the world's most sensitive cargo
    but he's not marked.
    Nowhere does his jacket say FRAGILE,
    HANDLE WITH CARE.

10   His ear fills up with breathing.
    He hears the hum of a boy's dream
    deep inside him.

    We're not going to be able
    to live in the world
15   if we're not willing to do what he's doing
    with one another.

    The road will only be wide.
    The rain will never stop falling.

Multiple-Choice Questions

31. In lines 1-5, what is the attitude of the man?

    A. He is annoyed because of the rain.

    B. He is concerned with his own welfare.

    C. He is rushing because he is late.

    D. He is protective of the sleeping boy.

32. In line 6, what does "the world's most sensitive cargo" refer to?

    A. a jacket

    B. the boy

    C. a box of fragile items

    D. the man

33. Lines 6-9 contain an example of

    A. alliteration.

    B. flashback.

    C. hyperbole.

    D. metaphor.

34. In lines 13-18, the image from the beginning of the poem comes to symbolize the relationship

    A. between children and adults.

    B. among the people of the world.

    C. between fathers and sons.

    D. between husbands and wives.

35. The title of this poem, "Shoulders," represents the idea of

    A. support.

    B. strength.

    C. parenthood.

    D. freedom.

36. The **main** idea that the poet expresses is that

   A. fathers must care for their sons.

   B. the world is a lonely place.

   C. people need to support and protect one another.

   D. people should be careful crossing streets.

Open-Response Question

37. In "Shoulders," how does the poet use symbolism to convey her ideas? Explain your answer using specific examples from the poem.

   _____

   _____

   _____

   _____

   _____

   _____

Once a slave, Frederick Douglass (1817-1895) went on to become a respected journalist and statesman. The following selection is an excerpt from one of his autobiographies. Read the excerpt carefully and then answer the questions that follow.

Narrative of the Life of Frederick Douglass
by Frederick Douglass

Very soon after I went to live with Mr. and Mrs. Auld, she very kindly commenced to teach me the A, B, C. After I had learned this, she assisted me in learning to spell words of three or four letters. Just at this point of my progress, Mr. Auld found out what was going on,
5 and at once forbade Mrs. Auld to instruct me further, telling her, among other things, that it was unlawful, as well as unsafe, to teach a slave to read. To use his own words, further, he said, "If you give a slave an inch, he will take an ell. A slave should know nothing but to obey his master—to do as he is told to do. Learning would *spoil* the best slave in the world. Now,"
10 said he, "if you teach that slave (speaking of myself) how to read, there would be no keeping him. It would forever unfit him to be a slave. He would at once become unmanageable, and of no value to his master. As to himself, it could do him no good, but a great deal of harm. It would make him discontented and unhappy." These words sank deep in my heart, stirred
15 up sentiments within that lay slumbering, and called into existence an entirely new train of thought. It was a new and special revelation, explaining dark and mysterious things, with which my youthful understanding had struggled, but struggled in vain. I now understood what had been to me a most perplexing difficulty—to wit, the white man's power
20 to enslave the black man. It was a grand achievement, and I prized it highly. From that moment, I understood the pathway from slavery to freedom. It was just what I wanted, and I got it at a time when I the least expected it. Whilst I was saddened by the thought of losing the aid of my kind mistress, I was gladdened by the invaluable instruction which, by the merest accident,
25 I had gained from my master. Though conscious of the difficulty of learning without a teacher, I set out with high hope, and a fixed purpose, at whatever cost of trouble, to learn how to read. The very decided manner with which he spoke, and strove to impress his wife the evil consequences of giving me instruction, served to convince me that he was deeply sensible of the truths
30 he was uttering. It gave me the best assurance that I might rely with the utmost confidence on the results which, he said, would flow from teaching me to read. What he most dreaded, that I most desired. What he most loved, that I most hated. That which to him was a great evil, to be carefully shunned, was to me a great good, to be diligently sought; and the argument
35 which he so warmly urged, against my learning to read, only served to inspire me with a desire and determination to learn. In learning to read, I owe almost as much to the bitter opposition of my master, as to the kindly aid of my mistress. I acknowledge the benefit of both.

Multiple-Choice Questions

38. Mr. Auld, Douglass's master,

    A. did not want Douglass to become educated.

    B. advised Douglass to learn as much as he could.

    C. taught Douglass the alphabet.

    D. encouraged Mrs. Auld to teach Douglass.

39. What was the "invaluable instruction" (line 24) that Douglass received from Mr. Auld?

    A. He learned to read.

    B. He came to recognize the value of hard work.

    C. He realized that education could pave the way to freedom.

    D. He learned to feel more contented with his situation.

40. The role that Mr. Auld played in inspiring Douglass is an example of

    A. irony.

    B. foreshadowing.

    C. allegory.

    D. satire.

41. In line 32, dreaded and desired are examples of

    A. adjectives.

    B. past tense.

    C. present participles.

    D. past participles.

Open-Response Question

42. Explain how the author uses a series of contrasts in lines 32-36 to get his point across. Use information from the excerpt to support your answer.

_____

_____

_____

_____

_____

_____

*As you read the following short story, think about the two main characters
and their relationship. When you have finished reading, answer the
questions that follow.*

Powder

by Tobias Wolff

1 Just before Christmas my father took me skiing at Mount Baker. He'd had to fight for the privilege of my company, because my mother was still angry with him for sneaking me into a night-club during our last visit, to see Thelonious Monk.

2 He wouldn't give up. He promised, hand on heart, to take good care of me and have me home for dinner on Christmas Eve, and she relented. But as we were checking out of the lodge that morning it began to snow, and in this snow he observed some quality that made it necessary for us to get in one last run. We got in several last runs. He was indifferent to my fretting. Snow whirled around us in bitter, blinding squalls, hissing like sand, and still we skied. As the lift bore us to the peak yet again, my father looked at his watch and said, "Criminey. This'll have to be a fast one."

3 By now I couldn't see the trail. There was no point in trying. I stuck to him like white on rice and did what he did and somehow made it to the bottom without sailing off a cliff. We returned our skis and my father put chains on the Austin-Healy while I swayed from foot to foot, clapping my mittens and wishing I were home. I could see everything. The green tablecloth, the plates with the holly pattern, the red candles waiting to be lit.

4 We passed a diner on our way out. "You want some soup?" my father asked. I shook my head. "Buck up," he said, "I'll get you there. Right, doctor?"

5 I was supposed to say, "Right, doctor," but I didn't say anything.

6 A state trooper waved us down outside the resort. A pair of sawhorses were blocking the road. The trooper came up to our car and bent down to my father's window. His face was bleached by the cold. Snowflakes clung to his eyebrows and to the fur trim of his jacket and cap.

7 "Don't tell me," my father said.

8 The trooper told him. The road was closed. It might get cleared, it might not. Storm took everyone by surprise. So much, so fast. Hard to get people moving. Christmas Eve. What can you do?

9 My father said, "Look. We're talking about four, five inches. I've taken this car through worse than that."

10 The trooper straightened up, boots creaking. His face was out of sight but I could hear him. "The road is closed."

11 My father sat with both hands on the wheel, rubbing the wood with his thumbs. He looked at the barricade for a long time. He seemed to be trying to master the idea of it. Then he thanked the trooper, and with a weird, old-maidy show of caution turned the car around. "Your mother will never forgive me for this," he said.

12 "We should have left before," I said. "Doctor."

13   He didn't speak to me again until we were both in a booth at the diner, waiting for our burgers. "She won't forgive me," he said. "Do you understand? Never."

14   "I guess," I said, but no guesswork was required; she wouldn't forgive him.

15   "I can't let that happen." He bent toward me. "I'll tell you what I want. I want us to be together again. Is that what you want?"

16   I wasn't sure, but I said, "Yes, sir."

17   He bumped my chin with his knuckles. "That's all I needed to hear."

18   When we finished eating he went to the pay phone in the back of the diner, then joined me in the booth again. I figured he'd called my mother, but didn't give a report. He sipped at his coffee and stared out the window at the empty road. "Come on!" when the trooper's car went past, lights flashing, he got up and dropped some money on the check. "Okay. *Vamanos.*"

19   The wind had died. The snow was falling straight down, less of it now, lighter. We drove away from the resort, right up to the barricade. "Move it," my father told me. When I looked at him he said, "What are you waiting for?" I got out and dragged one of the sawhorses aside, then pushed it back after he drove through. When I got inside the car he said, "Now you're an accomplice. We go down together." He put the car in gear and looked at me. "Joke, doctor."

20   "Funny, doctor."

21   Down the first long stretch I watched the road behind us, to see if the trooper was on our tail. The barricade vanished. Then there was nothing but snow: snow on the road, snow kicking up from the chains, snow on the trees, snow in the sky; and our trail in the snow. I faced around and had a shock. The lie of the road behind us had been marked by our own tracks, but there were no tracks ahead of us. My father was breaking virgin snow between a line of tall trees. He was humming "Stars Fell on Alabama." I felt snow brush along the floorboards under my feet. To keep my hands from shaking I clamped them between my knees.

22   My father grunted in a thoughtful way and said, "Don't ever try this yourself."

23   "I won't."

24   "That's what you say now, but someday you'll get your license and then you'll think you can do anything. Only you won't be able to do this. You need, I don't know—a certain instinct."

25   "Maybe I have it."

26   "You don't. You have strong points, but not . . . you know. I only mention it because I don't want you to get the idea this is something just anybody can do. I'm a great driver. That's not a virtue, okay? It's just a fact, and one you should be aware of. Of course you have to give the old heap some credit, too—there aren't many cars I'd try this with. Listen!"

27   I listened. I heard the slap of the chains, the stiff, jerky rasp of the wipers, the purr of the engine. It really did purr. The car was almost new. My father couldn't afford it, and kept promising to sell it, but here it was.

28   I said, "Where do you think that policeman went to?

"Are you warm enough?" He reached over and cranked up the blower. Then he turned off the wipers. We didn't need them. The clouds had brightened. A few sparse, feathery flakes drifted into our slipstream and were swept away. We left the trees and entered a broad field of snow that

29   ran level for a while and then tilted sharply downward. Orange stakes had been planted at intervals in two parallel lines and my father ran a course between them, though they were far enough apart to leave considerable doubt in my mind as to where exactly the road lay. He was humming again, doing little scat riffs around the melody.

30   "Okay, then. What are my strong points?"

31   "Don't get me started," he said. "It'd take all day."

32   "Oh, right. Name one."

33   "Easy. You always think ahead."

True. I always thought ahead. I was a boy who kept his clothes on numbered hangers to ensure proper rotation. I bothered my teachers for homework assignments far ahead of their due dates so I could make up schedules. I thought ahead, and that was why I knew that there would be other troopers waiting for us at the end of our ride, if we got there. What I

34   did not know was that my father would wheedle and plead his way past them—he didn't sing "O Tannenbaum" but just about—and get me home for dinner, buying a little more time before my mother decided to make the split final. I knew we'd get caught; I was resigned to it. And maybe for this reason I stopped moping and began to enjoy myself.

Why not? This was one for the books. Like being in a speedboat, only better. You can't go downhill in a boat. And it was all ours. And it kept coming, the laden trees, the unbroken surface of snow, the sudden white vistas. Here and there I saw hints of the road, ditches, fences, stakes, but

35   not so many that I could have found my way. But then I didn't have to. My father in his forty-eighth year, rumpled, kind, bankrupt of honor, flushed with certainty. He was a great driver. All persuasion, no coercion. Such subtlety at the wheel, such tactful pedalwork. I actually trusted him. And the best was yet to come—switchbacks and hairpins impossible to describe. Except maybe to say this: if you haven't driven fresh powder, you haven't driven.

Multiple-choice Questions

43. This story is told from what point of view?

    A. first person

    B. second person

    C. third person

    D. omniscient

44. The father's actions suggest that he is

    A. reliable.

    B. unfeeling.

    C. irresponsible.

    D. sensible.

45. When the father went to the telephone in the diner, it's likely that he

    A. called his wife.

    B. checked the chains on the car's tires.

    C. looked to see if the barricade was still there.

    D. phoned the police.

46. Which word is closest to the meaning of *wheedle* in paragraph 34?

    A. shout

    B. hurry

    C. fight

    D. coax

47. Based on the story, the way the father drives could be seen as symbolic of his

    A. love of his son.

    B. general way of living.

    C. attitude toward work.

    D. determination to stay married.

Open-Response Question

48. Describe the relationship between father and son. Support your answer with evidence from the story.

_____

_____

_____

_____

_____

_____

COMPOSITION

In many works of literature, one character has a significant effect on other characters. The effect may be good or bad, or it may be both.

Identify a work of literature that you have read in or out of class in which a main character significantly affects other characters. In an essay, describe the effects and explain why they are positive, negative, or a combination of both.

Index

Acknowledgments

Excerpt from *Gandhi: A Memoir* by William L. Shirer. © 1979 by William L. Shirer. A Washington Square Press Publication of Pocket Books, a Simon & Schuster Division of Gulf & Western Corporation. New York. Pages 11-12

Excerpt from *Living with Art* by Rita Gilbert. © 1992 by Rita Gilbert. All Rights Reserved. McGraw Hill, Inc. Pages 46-47

Excerpt from *The Old Man and the Sea* by Ernest Hemingway. © 1952 by Charles Scribner's Sons. New York. Page 49

Marine Animals at Risk from *Marine Science* by Thomas F. Greene. © 1998 Amsco School Publications, Inc. Page 63

Excerpt from the Apprentice from *Four Square* by Dorothy Canfield Fisher. © 1947 by Curtis Publishing Company and renewed 1975 by Downe Publishing, Inc. Reprinted by permission of Harcourt, Brace & Company. Page 66

Excerpt from *What I Have Lived For* from Autobiography of Bertrand Russell by Bertrand Russell. © 1967. Reprinted by permission Routledge Ltd. Pages 71-72

"The Sword of Damocles" from *The Book of Virtues for Young People* by William J. Bennett. Published by Silver Burdett Press, Simon & Schuster Education Group. Used by permission. Pages 74-75

"Sound Minds in Healthy Bodies" from *Western Civilization* by Gerson Antell and Walter Harris. © 1983 Amsco School Publications, Inc. Page 83

"Bird Girl" by Clark Deleon. © 1987 by *The Philadelphia Inquirer.* Reprinted by permission. Pages 91-92

"The Courage That My Mother Had" from *Collected Poems* by Edna St. Vincent Millay. © 1954, 1982 by Norma Millay Ellis. Reprinted by permission of Elizabeth Barnett, literary executor. Harper Collins Publishers.

"Will Global Warming Cause a Meltdown?" from *Marine Science* by Thomas F. Greene. © 1998 by Amsco School Publications, Inc. Page 102

"Love! Who'd Have Guessed It?" by Cheryl Dale. Reprinted courtesy of *Teen Magazine.* Pages 104-105

"Shooting Hoops" by William G. Christ. © William G. Christ. Pages 108-109

"Stirring Up Trouble" by Stephen S. Morse. Reprinted by permission of *The Sciences* and is from the September/October 1990 issue. Pages 111-112

"Jabberwocky" by Lewis Carroll. Page 116

"The Discovery of Coca-Cola" from *The Big Drink: The Story of Coca-Cola* by E.J. Kahn, Jr. © 1950, 1959, 1960. Reprinted by permission of Random House. Pages 125-126

"To Create Another Earth, or Let It Be" by Seth Borenstein. *KRT News Service.* Pages 128-129

"The Rewards of Living a Solitary Life" by May Sarton. From *The New York Times,* April 6, 1974 © 1974 by The New York Times Company. Reprinted by permission. Pages 142-143

"Progress" from *Barbed Wire* by John Sterling Harris © 1974. Brigham University Press. Reprinted with permission by the Author. Page 146

"Apartment House" by Gerald Raftery. © Gerald Raftery. Page 147

"Rambos of the Road" by Martin Gottfried. From *Newsweek* 9/8/86. Reprinted by permission of Martin Gottfried. Page 160

"Hunger of Memory" from *Hunger of Memory* by Richard Rodriguez. © 1982 by Richard Rodriguez. Reprinted by permission of David R. Godine, Publisher. Pages 164-165

"Mother to Son" by Langston Hughes. © 1926 by Alfred A. Knopf, Inc., and renewed 1954 by Langston Hughes. Reprinted from *Selected Poems of Langston Hughes* by permission of Alfred A. Knopf, Inc. Page 168

"The Story of an Hour" by Kate Chopin. Page 170

"Caged Bird" from *I Know Why the Caged Bird Sings* by Maya Angelou. © 1969 Random House. Copyright renewed 1996.

"Arachne" as told by Olivia Coolidge. From *Pageants.* © 1986. The Houghton Mifflin Company. Page 186

Dictionary entries reprinted from *Merriam-Webster's Collegiate Dictionary,* Tenth Edition. © 1993 Merriam-Webster, Inc. Pages 197, 203, 207, 254

"You're Short, Besides" by Sucheng Chan. First published in *Making Waves: An Anthology of Writings By and About Asian Women.* © 1989 by Asian Women United of California. Reprinted by permission of Beacon Press. Pages 204-205

Excerpt from "To Build a Fire" by Jack London. Pages 211 and 241

Excerpt from *Silent Spring* by Rachel Carson. © 1962 by Rachel Carson. Renewed 1990 by Roger Christie. Reprinted by permission of Houghton Mifflin Company. All rights reserved. Pages 247-248

"Dead Men's Path" from *Girls at War and Other Stories* by Chinua Achebe. © 1972, 1973 by Chinua Achebe. Used by permission of Doubleday, a division of Bantam Doubleday Dell Publishing Group, Inc. Pages 251-252

Excerpt From " I Have a Dream" by Martin Luther King, Jr. Reprinted by arrangement with the heirs of the Estate of Martin Luther King, Jr., c/o Writer's House, Inc. as agents for the proprietor. © 1963 by Martin Luther King, Jr. Copyright renewed 1991 by Coretta Scott King. Page 255

"Tea Party" from *Improvisation in Creative Drama* by Betty Keller. © 1988 by Meriweather Publishing Ltd. 885 Elkton Drive, Colorado Springs, CO 80907. Used by permission. Pages 258-261

Excerpt from the *Story of My Life* by Helen Keller © 1954. Used by permission of Doubleday, a division of Bantam Doubleday Dell Publishing Group, Inc. Pages 264-265

"Shoulders" by Naomi Shihab Nye. © Naomi Shihab Nye. Page 268

Excerpt from *Narrative of the Life of Frederick Douglass* by Frederick Douglass. Page 271

"Powder" from *The Night in Question* by Tobias Wolff. © 1996 by Tobias Wolff. Reprinted by permission of Alfred A. Knopf, Inc. Pages 274-276